# 24-HOUR baby QUILTS

Linda Causee

LEISURE ARTS®
the art of everyday living
Little Rock, Arkansas

Produced by The Creative Partners™, LLC

**Produced by**

CREATIVE PARTNERS LLC

**Production Team**

*Creative Directors:* Rita Weiss and
 Jean Leinhauser

*Editorial Director:* Linda Causee

*Photography:* Carol Wilson Mansfield

*Technical Editing:* Ann Harnden,
 Christina Wilson

*Book Design:* Linda Causee

*Pattern Testers:* Hope Adams,
 Patricia Bliss, Shirley Cushing,
 Linda Ferguson, Ann Harnden,
 Cathy Howell, Dawn Kallunki,
 Wanda MacLachlan, and
 April McArthur

*Machine Quilting:* Linda Ferguson and
 Faith Horsky

*The following companies supplied
their products for the projects in this
book:*

Fairfield Processing Corp.:
 Machine 60/40 Blend®

Northcott Silks, Inc.:
 Candy Store

**Published by Leisure Arts**

LEISURE ARTS
*the art of everyday living*

# Introduction

You've just learned that your favorite aunt is about to have her first grandchild and you—as the only quilt maker in the family—will be expected to make a quilt for the baby shower next week. You'd love to do it, but the deadline looms for a quilt you're making for an international competition, you've promised to chaperone a soccer field trip, and you've volunteered to help with your church's bake sale. What to do now?

This book is your answer because here are 20 delightful baby quilts you can make in less than 24 hours each! Choose your favorite quilt, get out your rotary cutter, your stash of fabric and your sewing machine. Then just follow our easy step-by-step instructions and in a few hours you'll have an adorable quilt completely finished!

To help you choose your quilt, I've given you the time that it took me to complete each quilt. If you have only nine hours for quilt making, try the Little League Quilt on page 52. Or if you have lots of time, try Lost in the Stars on page 69. Any of the quilts will make a treasured gift.

Of course you don't have to spend 24 straight hours on the quilt! You can take four days of six hours, or three 8-hour days, or just squeeze in an hour here and there. Making a quilt shouldn't be a chore, there's no prize for the quilter who finishes first. If it takes longer than the suggested time, that's okay too.

If you've forgotten how to make a quilt—or if you're a beginner—just read the section on General Directions which begins on page 132. While it doesn't tell you everything you need to know about quilt making, it does have everything you need to know about making these very special baby quilts.

And can you think of a better way to spend 24 hours than creating a beautiful quilt to welcome a precious baby into the world? You'll be giving more than a quilt—you'll be giving an heirloom full of precious memories.

# Contents

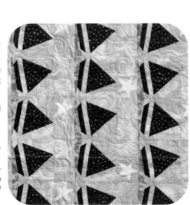

Candy Pinwheels, 72

Baking Cookies, 84

Baby's Crazy Quilt, 116

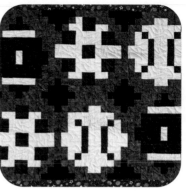

Sports Balls Postage Stamps, 126

Lost in the Stars, 68

Baby Prints, 80

Baby's Favorite Things, 112

Baby's Garden, 56

My Baby Genius, 76

Now I Know My Numbers and ABCs, 88

Hearts and Flowers Postage Stamps, 120

As soon as I saw this novelty print fabric filled with baby bunnies, I knew that it would make a wonderful quilt for a little one. What little child doesn't love bunnies, especially bunnies as busy as these?

Busy bunnies are doing all the things that any child would love to do: playing baseball, riding in a car, flying kites, flying in an airplane, riding in a rocket, ice skating and more. To accent the fun, I've added the colorful pinwheels to fill the quilt with even more excitement.

The child who receives this quilt may not be able to do all of the bunny activities, but wrapped in this quilt on a visit to dreamland will make it all seem real.

# Busy Baby Bunnies

## APPROXIMATE SIZE
42" x 54"

## BLOCK SIZE
12" x 12" finished

## TECHNIQUE
Foundation Piecing

## MATERIALS
\*1 yard novelty print or baby print (If using a novelty print, squares need to be 6½" square.)

¾ yard light blue

¾ yard dark blue

½ yard green

½ yard red

1½ yards cream

½ yard binding

3 yards backing

Batting

## PATTERNS
Rectangle (page 11)
Square (page 11)

## CUTTING
Note: Pieces for foundation piecing do not have to be cut to exact sizes. Read pages 133 to 138 before beginning. If you do not want to use foundation piecing, cut the following pieces.

### Blocks

12 squares, 6½" x 6½", novelty print (A)

48 squares, 3½" x 3½", light blue (B)

40 squares, 37⁄8" x 37⁄8", dark blue, cut in half diagonally (C)

40 squares, 23⁄8" x 23⁄8", green, cut in half diagonally (D)

12 squares, 4¼" x 4¼", red, cut in quarters diagonally (F)

48 rectangles, 3½" x 6½", cream (G)

24 squares, 23⁄8" x 23⁄8", cream, cut in half diagonally (H)

Pieced Border
16 squares, 3⅞" x 3⅞", dark blue (cut in half diagonally)
16 squares, 2⅜" x 2⅜", green
3 squares, 4¼" x 4¼", red (cut in quarters diagonally)
16 squares, 2⅜" x 2⅜", cream
14 rectangles, 2⅜" x 2⅜", cream
14 rectangles, 3½" x 6½", cream

Finishing
6 strips, 2½"-wide, binding

# INSTRUCTIONS

**Note:** *Read Foundation Piecing, pages 133 to 138, before beginning.*

1. Make 80 Square and 48 Rectangle foundations using patterns on page 11. (**Diagram 1**)

**Diagram 1**

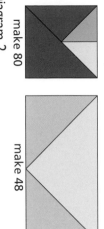

2. Make Squares and Rectangles using foundation piecing. (**Diagram 2**)

**Hint:** *Write fabric colors on foundations to make piecing easier.*

**Diagram 2**

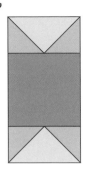

make 80    make 48

3. For blocks, sew a pieced Rectangle to opposite sides of a 6½" novelty print square. (**Diagram 3**)

**Diagram 3**

4. Sew a pieced Square to opposite sides of a pieced Rectangle, noting position. (**Diagram 4**) Repeat.

**Diagram 4**

5. Sew units made in step 4 to top and bottom of unit made in step 3 to complete a Star block. (**Diagram 5**) Make 12 blocks.

**Diagram 5**

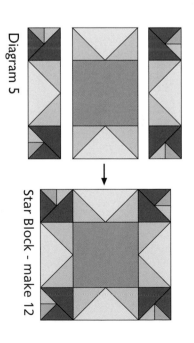

Star Block - make 12

6. For pieced border, sew a pieced Square to opposite short sides of 3½" x 6½" cream rectangle noting position. (**Diagram 6**) Make 14 border units. You will have four pieced Squares left over.

**Diagram 6**

**Note:** *If you do not want to use foundation piecing, make Star block referring to* **Diagram A.**

**Diagram A**

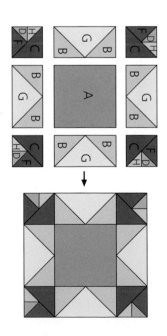

7. Place blocks in four rows of three blocks with a Border Unit at each end of each row noting position. (Diagram 7)

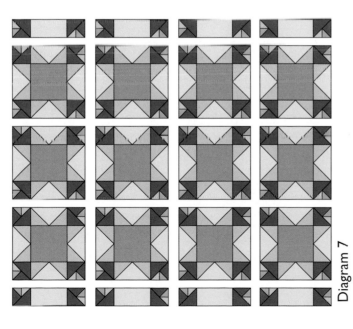

Diagram 7

8. Sew three Border Units together; sew a pieced Square to each end. Repeat. (Diagram 8)

Diagram 8

9. Sew to top and bottom of quilt top. (Diagram 9)

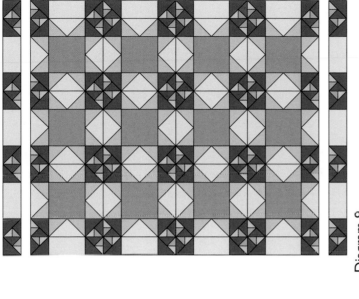

Diagram 9

10. Refer to Finishing, pages 138 to 142, to complete your quilt.

9

Busy Baby Bunnies Quilt Layout

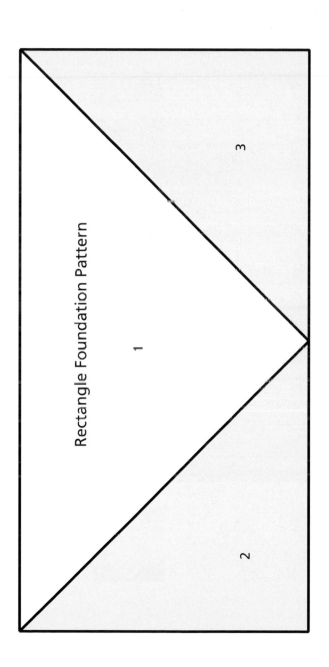

Rectangle Foundation Pattern

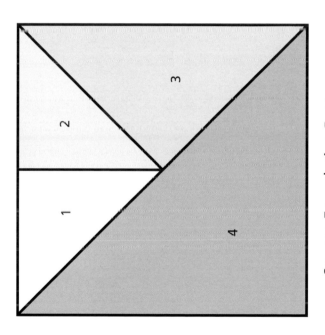

Square Foundation Pattern

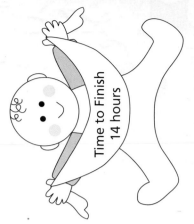

# For Baby's Christening

*The perfect gift for the newborn baby: a beautiful blanket to hold the baby at his or her Christening. This soft pastel quilt is enhanced with angels, crosses, hearts and stars.*

*The quilt is easily made with simple nine-patch blocks created with white and cream fabrics. The fused Easy Appliqué squares are placed between the nine-patch blocks.*

*The finished quilt looks as if it has taken forever to complete. Only you will know that it took you less than a day to make this quilt that will surely become a family heirloom.*

## APPROXIMATE SIZE
41¹/₂" x 46¹/₂"

## BLOCK SIZES
Nine-Patch block, 4¹/₂" x 4¹/₂" finished
Cross block, 4¹/₂" x 9" finished
Angel block, 9" x 9" finished
Hearts and Stars blocks, 4¹/₂" x 4¹/₂" finished

## TECHNIQUES
Strip Piecing, Easy Appliqué

## MATERIALS
1³/₄ yards white (includes second border and binding)
1¹/₄ yards cream (includes first border)
Scraps of assorted pastels (blue, pink, yellow)
1 yard lightweight paper-backed fusible web
1¹/₂ yards backing
Batting
Invisible thread

## PATTERNS
Hearts (page 16)
Stars (page 16)
Angel (page 17)
Cross (page 17)

## CUTTING
### Blocks
3 strips, 2"-wide, white (Nine-Patch blocks)
3 strips, 2" x 20", white (Nine-Patch blocks)
3 strips, 2"-wide, cream (Nine-Patch blocks)
3 strips, 2" x 20", cream (Nine-Patch blocks)
12 squares, 5" x 5", white (Hearts and Stars blocks)
2 rectangles, 5" x 9¹/₂", cream (Cross blocks)
2 squares, 9¹/₂" x 9¹/₂", cream (Angel blocks)

### Finishing
4 strips, 2"-wide, cream (first border)
5 strips, 3"-wide, white (second border)
5 strips, 2¹/₂"-wide, white (binding)

# INSTRUCTIONS

## Nine-Patch Blocks

1. For strip set 1, sew a 2"-wide cream strip to each side of a 2"-wide white strip. Repeat. (**Diagram 1**) Press seams to one side.

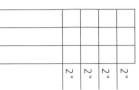

**Diagram 1**

2. For strip set 2, sew a 2"-wide white strip to each side of a 2"-wide cream strip. (**Diagram 2**) Press seams in opposite direction.

**Diagram 2**

3. Repeat steps 1 and 2 with remaining 2"-wide white and cream strips. Cut all strip sets at 2" intervals. (**Diagram 3**)

4. Cut all strip sets at 2" intervals. (**Diagram 3**)

**Diagram 3**

5. For Nine-Patch A, sew a strip set 1 unit to opposite sides of a strip set 2 unit. (**Diagram 4**) Make 16 Nine-Patch A.

Nine-patch A
make 16

**Diagram 4**

6. For Nine-Patch B, sew a strip set 2 unit to opposite sides of a strip set 1 unit. (**Diagram 5**) Make 16 Nine-Patch B.

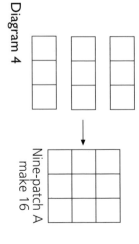

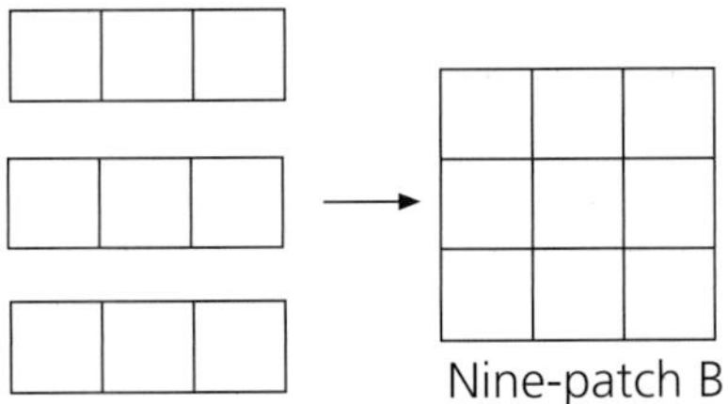

Nine-patch B
make 16

**Diagram 5**

## Appliqué Blocks

1. Trace patterns (pages 16 to 17) for appliqué pieces onto paper side of fusible web. You will need enough Hearts for six Heart blocks, Stars for six Star blocks, Crosses for two Cross blocks and Angels for two Angel blocks.

2. Rough-cut pattern shapes and press to wrong sides of fabrics as follows: Stars and Angel Hair on yellow, Hearts and Angel Face and Hands on pink, Crosses and Angel Wings on white, and Angel dress and sleeves on blue.

3. Cut out all pattern shapes along traced lines. Keep paper on pieces until ready to use.

4. Position Stars on 5" x 5" white squares and press to fuse. Make six Star blocks. (**Diagram 6**)

**Diagram 6**

make 6

5. Position Hearts on 5" x 5" white squares and press to fuse. **(Diagram 7)** Make six Heart blocks.

Diagram 7

6. Position Cross on 5" x 9½" cream rectangle and press to fuse. **(Diagram 8)** Repeat for another Cross block.

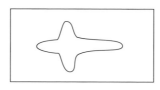

make 2

Diagram 8

7. Position Angel pieces on 9½" x 9½" cream square and press to fuse. **(Diagram 9)** Repeat for another Angel block.

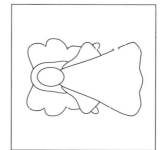

make 2

Diagram 9

8. Using invisible monofilament thread and a machine zigzag, stitch along raw edges of all appliqué pieces.

*Finishing*

1. Sew blocks together in sections referring to **Diagram 10**.

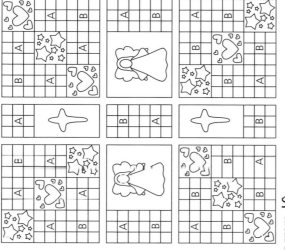

Diagram 10

2. Sew sections together. **(Diagram 11)**

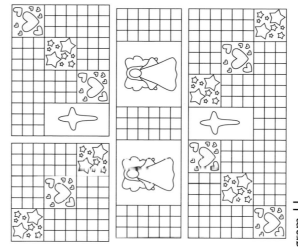

Diagram 11

3. Measure quilt top lengthwise; cut two 2"-wide cream strips to that length. Sew to sides of quilt. Measure quilt top crosswise; sew and cut two 2"-wide cream strips to that length. Sew to top and bottom of quilt.

4. Repeat step 3 for second border using 3"-wide white strips.

5. Refer to Finishing, pages 138 to 142, to complete your quilt.

15

Hearts Appliqué Pattern

Stars Appliqué Pattern

For Baby's Christening Quilt Layout

16

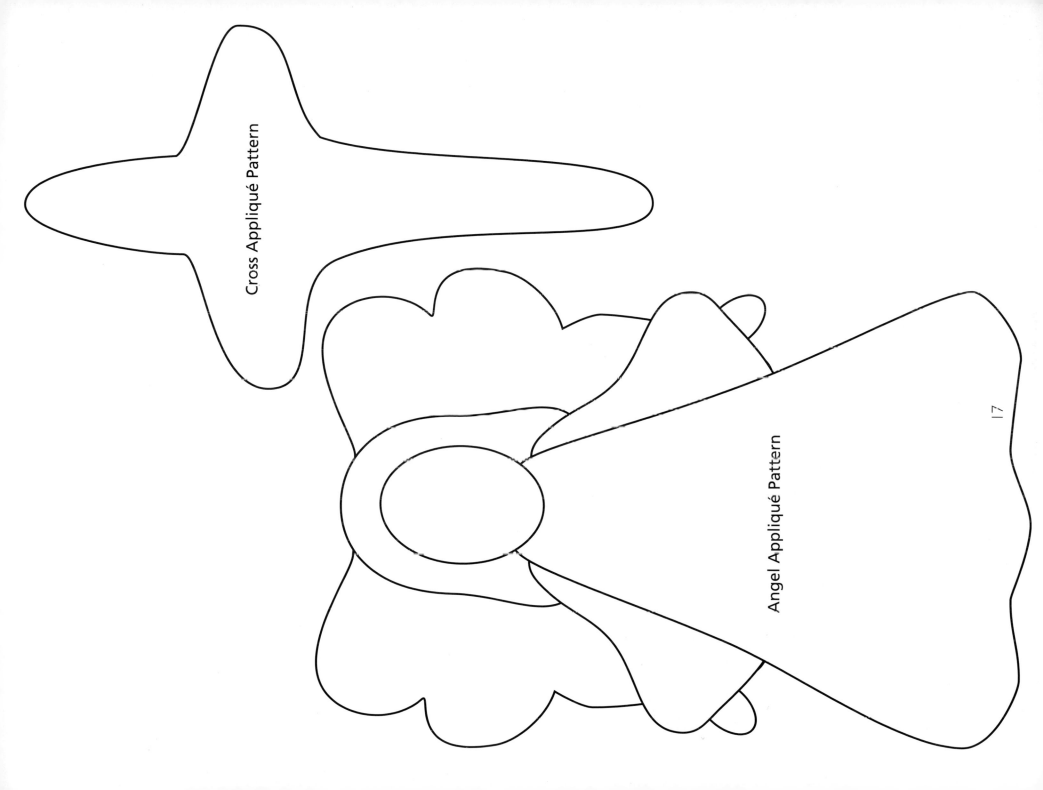

Cross Appliqué Pattern

Angel Appliqué Pattern

17

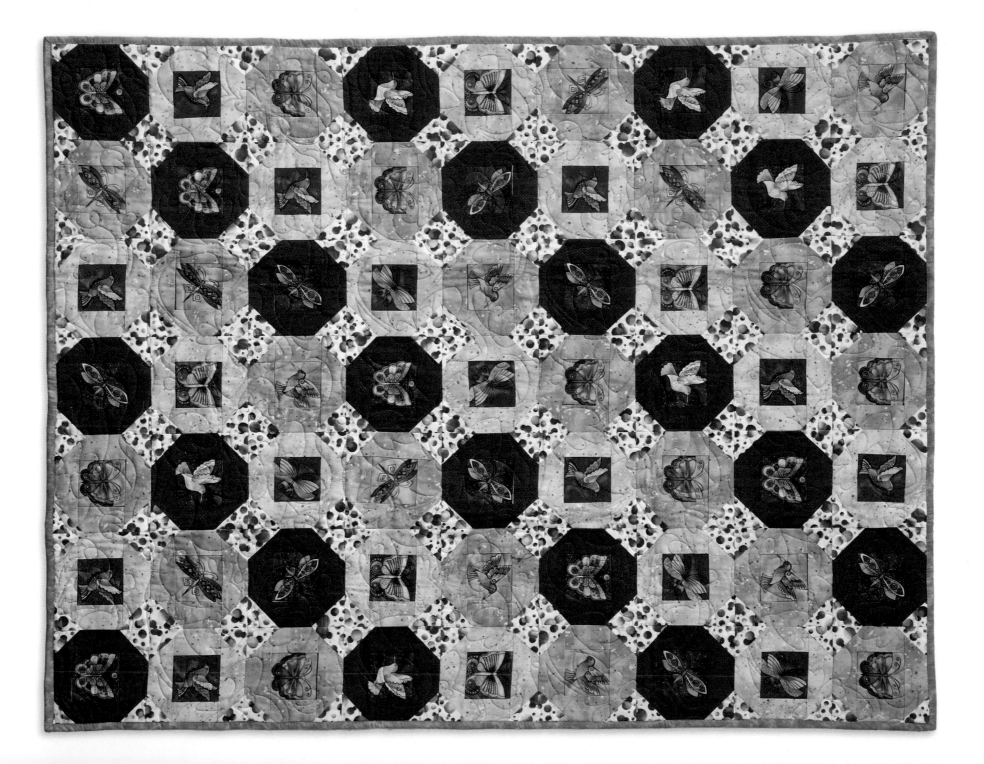

# Baby Birds & Butterflies

The hardest part about making this quilt is finding a novelty print that contains the flying creatures.

Once you have found it, buy enough fabric (about a yard) to fill up 63 "picture frames". Now using the foundation method (see page 133), make the 63 blocks, join them, and you have created a quilt in just a few hours that a child will love forever.

**APPROXIMATE SIZE**
42" x 54"

**BLOCK SIZE**
6" x 6" finished

**TECHNIQUE**
Foundation Piecing

**MATERIALS**
1 yard novelty print (need enough fabric for 63 squares, 3½" x 3½")
½ yard blue print
½ yard green print
½ yard pink print
1 yard white print
½ yard binding
2½ yards backing
Batting

**PATTERN**
Picture Frame Foundation (page 21)

**CUTTING**
Blocks

**Note:** *Even though you do not need to cut exact pieces for foundation piecing, below are measurements for cutting exact pieces. If you do not want to use foundation piecing, cut the following pieces.*

63 squares, 3½" x 3½", novelty print
42 rectangles, 2" x 3½", green print
42 rectangles, 2" x 6½", green print
42 rectangles, 2" x 3½", blue print
42 rectangles, 2" x 6½", blue print
42 rectangles, 2" x 3½", pink print
42 rectangles, 2" x 6½", pink print
126 squares, 3" x 3", white (cut in half diagonally)

Finishing

5 strips, 2½"-wide strips, (binding)

19

# INSTRUCTIONS

## Blocks

1. Make 63 foundations referring to Preparing the Foundation, page 133.

2. Make 21 Picture Frame blocks of each color combination referring to Making a Foundation-pieced block, pages 134 to 138. (**Diagram 1**)

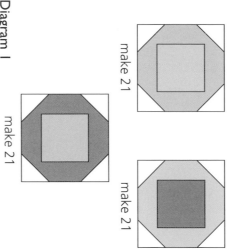

make 21

make 21

make 21

**Diagram 1**

2. Refer to Finishing, pages 138 to 142, to complete your quilt.

**Baby Birds and Butterflies Quilt Layout**

## Finishing

1. Place blocks in nine rows of seven blocks each. To simplify sewing, divide the blocks into sections. (**Diagram 2**) Sew each section, then sew sections together to complete quilt top.

**Diagram 2**

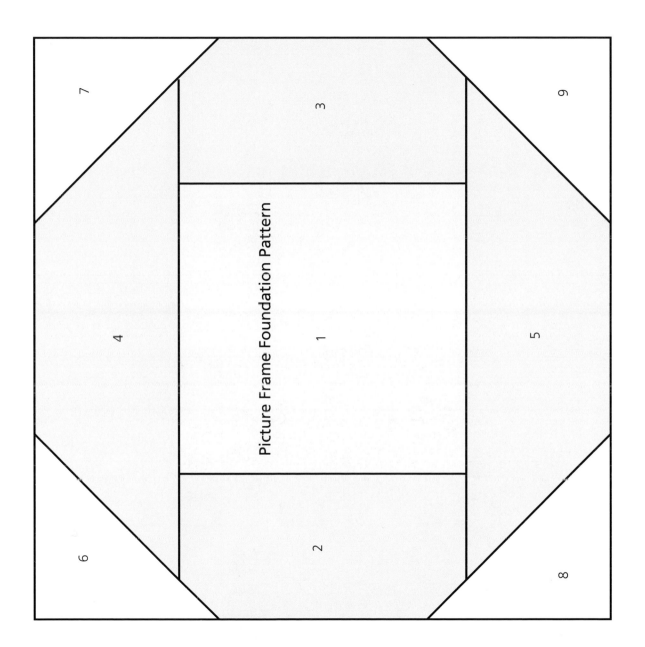

Picture Frame Foundation Pattern

1

2

3

4

5

6

7

8

9

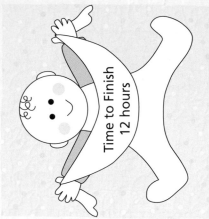

Time to Finish
12 hours

Little Kate's nursery school teacher taught Kate to sew by inviting her to outline with needle and thread the clever drawings the teacher had put on fabric. Once the drawing had been outlined with thread, Kate enjoyed coloring in the picture she had created.

Delighted with her work, Kate presented the sewing to her grandmother with the announcement, "Look, I can sew too."

When the proud grandmother showed me Kate's work, I knew I had to put the blocks into a quilt so that Kate might have a momento of her achievement. Since all of the blocks were not the same size, some of them had to have borders attached to make them all even. Simple appliqué blocks repeating the themes in the sewing characters were used to fill up the space.

And for the final touch, a series of gold stars for Kate's good work.

# Kate's Quilt

**APPROXIMATE SIZE**
41" x 52"

**BLOCK SIZE**
9" x 9" finished

**TECHNIQUES**
Easy Appliqué, Stitch and Flip

**MATERIALS**
3/8 yard blue
3/8 yard orange
3/8 yard light pink
7/8 yard blue print (sashing)
5/8 yard yellow
Scraps of assorted fabric colors
5/8 yard pink print (border)
1/2 yard binding
1 5/8 yard backing
Batting
Pearl cotton
Crayons
1/2 yard lightweight paper-backed fusible web
Invisible monofilament thread
Freezer paper (optional)

**PATTERNS**
Flower (page 27)
Rose (page 26)
Fish (page 28)
Heart (page 26)
Kitty (page 29)
Butterfly (page 29)

## CUTTING

### Blocks

**Note:** *Some of the blocks in the photographed quilt are made up of a smaller center surrounded by strips to make blocks the correct size.*

4 squares, 9½" x 9½", blue
4 squares, 9½" x 9½", orange
4 squares, 9½" x 9½", light pink

### Finishing

31 strips, 2½" x 9½", blue print (sashing)
20 squares, 2½" x 2½", yellow (cornerstones)
124 squares, 1½" x 1½", yellow (triangles)
5 strips, 3½"-wide, pink print (border)
5 strips, 2½"-wide, binding

# INSTRUCTIONS

### Blocks

1. For the child's picture blocks, trace patterns onto right side of 9½" x 9½" squares. **Note:** *Some of the original blocks were smaller than the others, so strips were added so all blocks were the same size.* Color the pictures with crayons, then outline with the Running stitch and pearl cotton. (**Diagram 1**) Heat-set the crayons to the block by placing a press cloth over the drawing and iron for a few seconds.

**Hint:** *Iron blocks onto shiny side of freezer paper to give the fabric more stability when coloring. Remove paper to stitch.*

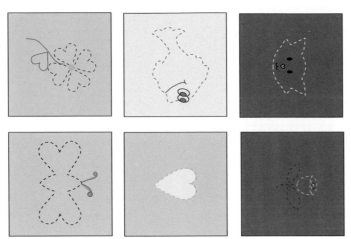

**Diagram 1**

2. For the appliqué blocks, trace patterns onto paper side of fusible web. Rough cut shapes and fuse onto wrong side of chosen fabric scraps. Cut out pieces along drawn lines.

3. Remove paper from shapes and position pattern pieces onto 9½" x 9½" squares; fuse in place. (**Diagram 2**) Outline shapes using clear monofilament thread and a small machine zigzag.

**Diagram 2**

### Finishing

1. For sashing strips, place a 1½" x 1½" yellow square right sides together with blue print 1½" x 9½" strip. (**Diagram 3**)

**Diagram 3**

2. Sew diagonally through yellow square. (**Diagram 4**)

**Hint:** *To help with sewing, draw a diagonal line on wrong side of 1½" x 1½" yellow squares. Then sew along drawn line.*

**Diagram 4**

3. Trim about 1/4" from stitching. (Diagram 5)

**Diagram 5**

4. Press open resulting triangle. (Diagram 6)

**Diagram 6**

5. Repeat along remaining three corners. (Diagram 7)

**Diagram 7**

6. Repeat steps 1 to 5 for remaing 2½" x 9½" blue print sashing strips.

7. For rows 1, 3, 5, 7, and 9, alternate blue print sashing strips and 2½" x 2½" yellow squares. For rows 2, 4, 6, and 8, alternate sashing strips and blocks. Refer to layout and photograph for placement.

8. Sew sashing rows and block rows, then sew rows together. (Diagram 8)

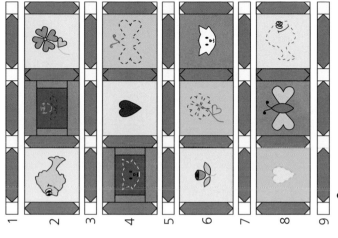

**Diagram 8**

9. Measure quilt lengthwise. Sew and cut two 3½"-wide pink print strips to that length; sew to sides of quilt. Measure quilt crosswise. Sew and cut two 3½"-wide pink print strips to that length; sew to top and bottom of quilt.

10. Refer to Finishing, pages 138 to 142, to complete your quilt.

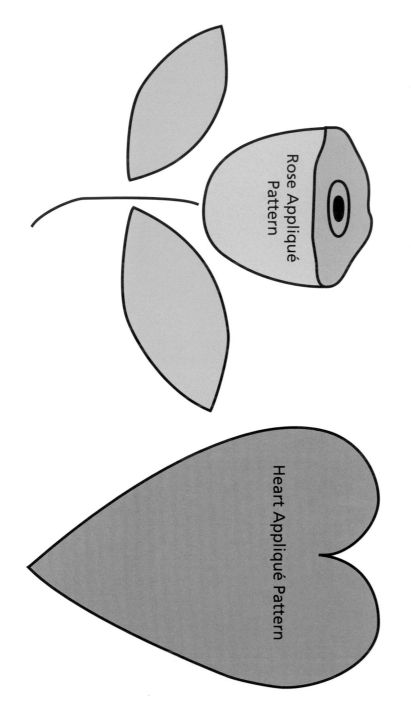

Rose Appliqué
Pattern

Heart Appliqué Pattern

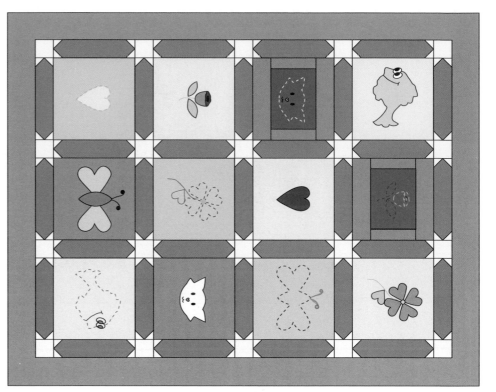

Flower Appliqué Pattern

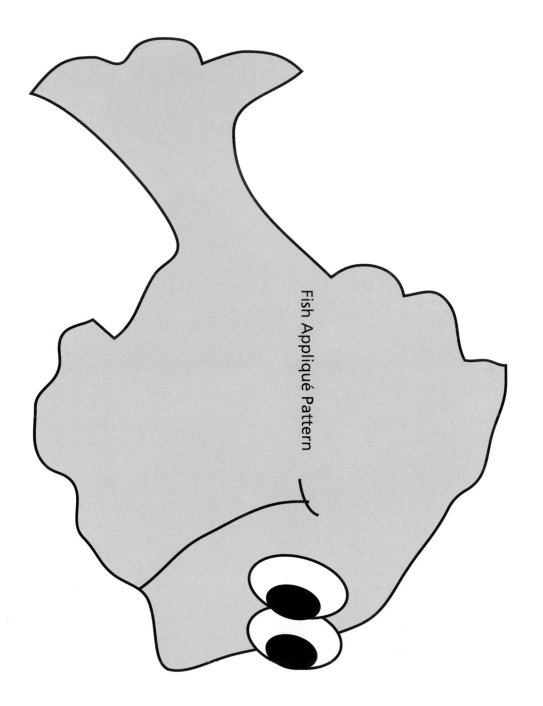

Fish Appliqué Pattern

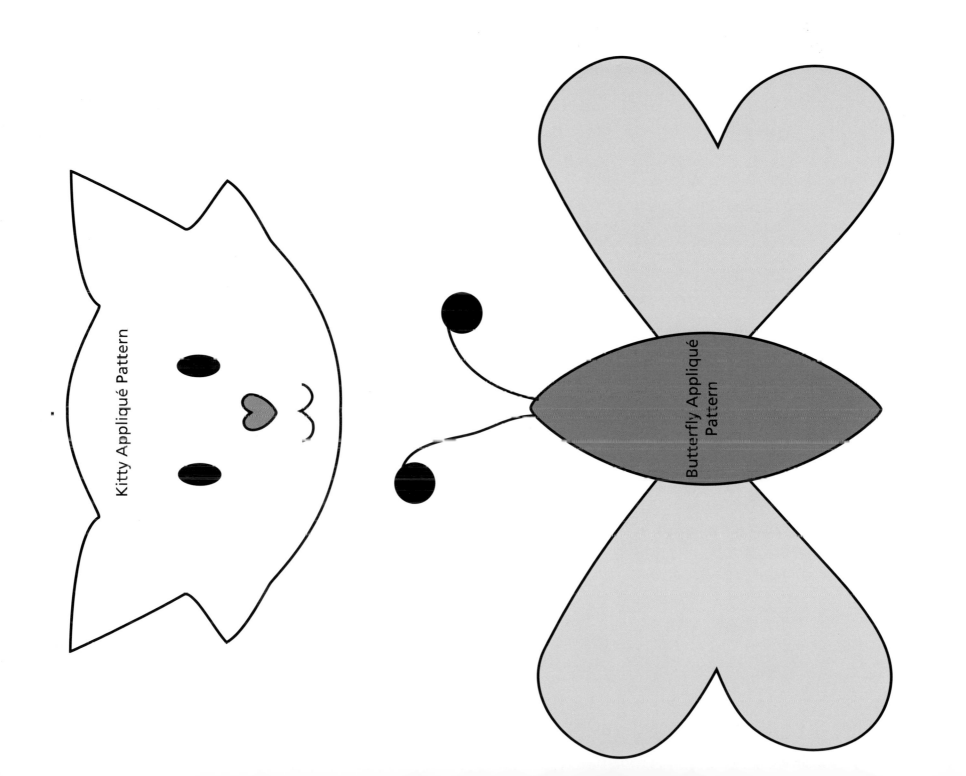

Kitty Appliqué Pattern

Butterfly Appliqué Pattern

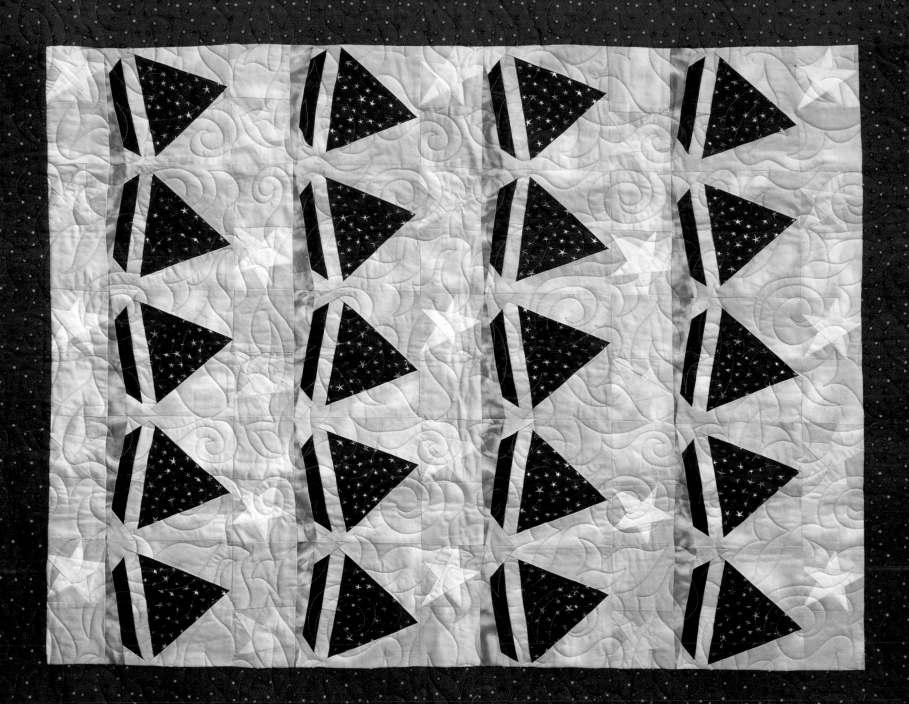

**Time to Finish 23 1/2 hours**

# Sail Off to Dreamland

*A floatilla of bright red sailboats make their way across this quilt, luring the lucky sleeping child to Dreamland. Rows of shining stars in the sky lead the way.*

*The use of foundation piecing makes this quilt so easy to complete, you'll want to make one for every child in your life. By working with the two Sailboat Foundation blocks, you create the illusion of boats moving in the water, rocking back and forth as the waves take them off to far-away places.*

*A quilt that's sure to please every little sailor!*

**APPROXIMATE SIZE**
36" x 45"

**BLOCK SIZE**
Star blocks, 3" x 3" finished
Sailboats, 6" x 6" finished

**TECHNIQUE**
Foundation Piecing

**MATERIALS**
1/3 yard red star print 1
1 1/2 yards light blue
1/8 yard medium blue
Scrap light brown
1/3 yard yellow
1/3 yard white
1/8 yard aqua
5/8 yard red star print 2 (border)
1/2 yard binding
1 1/2 yards backing
Batting

**PATTERNS**
Sailboat A Foundation (page 34)
Sailboat B Foundation (page 35)
Star A Foundation (page 34)
Star B Foundation (page 35)

**CUTTING**

**Blocks**

**Note:** *You do not have to cut exact pieces for foundation piecing.*

**Finishing**
25 squares, 3 1/2" x 3 1/2", light blue
4 strips, 3 1/2"-wide, red star print 2 (border)
4 strips, 2 1/2"-wide, binding

# INSTRUCTIONS

## Blocks

1. Referring to Preparing the Foundation, page 133, make foundations for 15 Star A, 10 Star B, 10 Sailboat A and 10 Sailboat B. (**Diagram 1**)

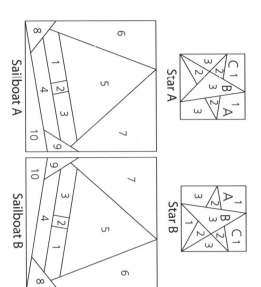

Star A

Sailboat A

Star B

Sailboat B

**Diagram 1**

2. Make blocks referring to Making a Foundation-pieced Block, pages 134 to 138. (**Diagram 2**)

**Note**: *Make six yellow Star A, nine white Star A, six yellow Star B and four white Star B.*

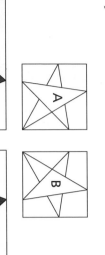

A

B

**Diagram 2**

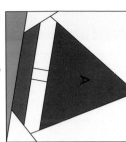

## Finishing

1. Place Star blocks alternating with 3¹/₂" x 3¹/₂" light blue squares for rows 1, 3, 5, 7 and 9. Place Sailboat blocks, alternating A and B, for rows 2, 4, 6 and 8. (**Diagram 3**)

2. Sew blocks together in rows, then sew rows together.

3. Measure quilt lengthwise. Cut 3¹/₂"-wide red star print 2 strips to that length; sew to sides of quilt. Measure quilt crosswise. Cut 3¹/₂"-wide red star print 2 strips to that length; sew to top and bottom of quilt.

4. Refer to Finishing, pages 138 to 142, to complete your quilt.

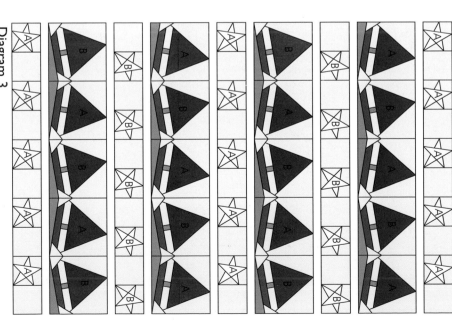

**Diagram 3**

32

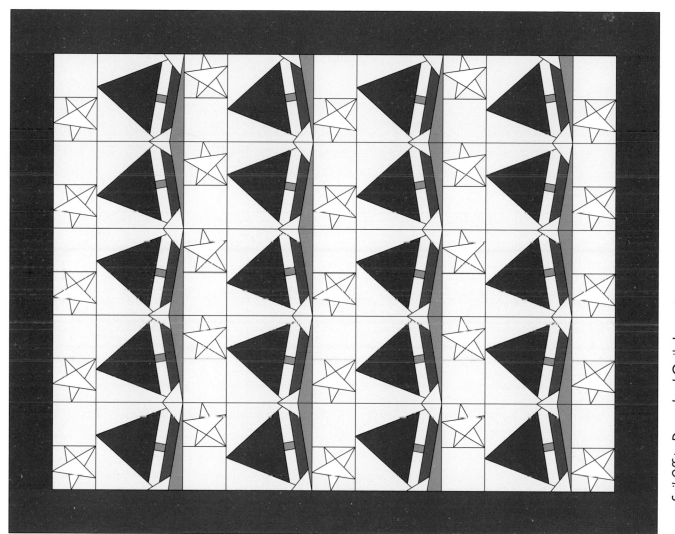

*Sail Off to Dreamland Quilt Layout*

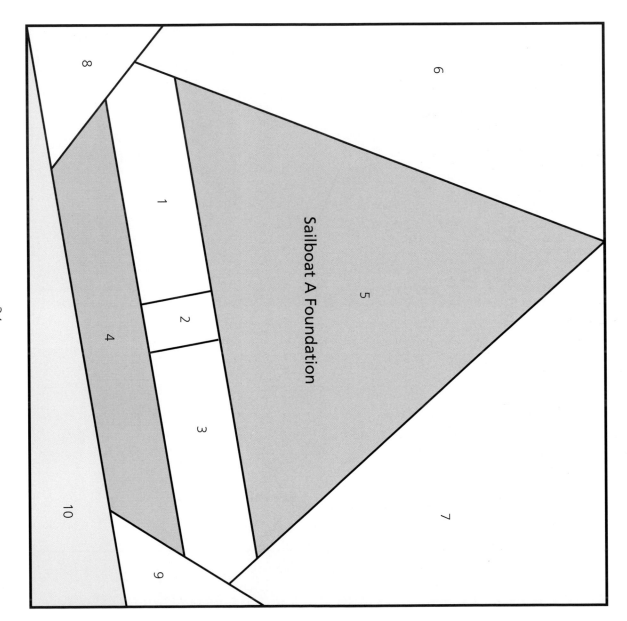

Sailboat A Foundation

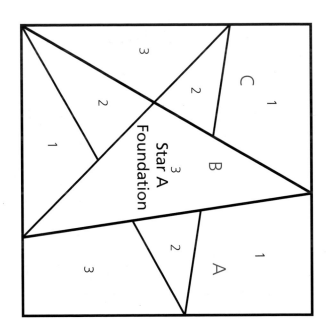

Star A Foundation

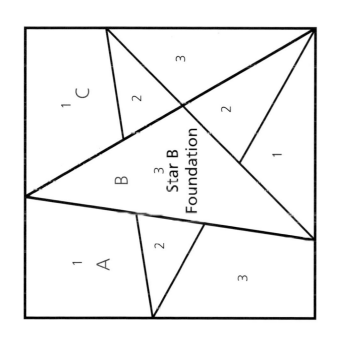

Star B
Foundation

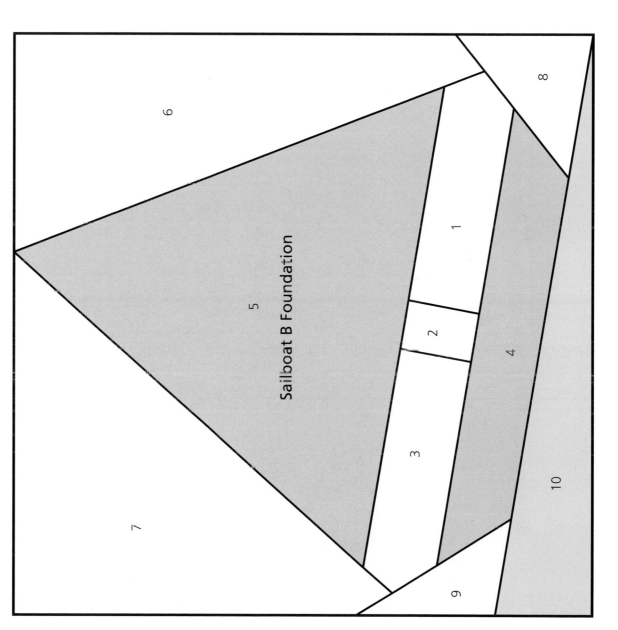

Sailboat B Foundation

# Angel Ribbons

I collect anything that harbors an angel: angel embroidery, angel statuary, and angel pictures. So, of course, I have angel fabrics in my stash. Not only did I have one angel fabric, but I happened to have a yard of two different prints from the same fabric line.

Those angel novelty prints were the inspiration for this quilt where the angel novelty print became the ribbons moving across the quilt. If angels aren't in your collection, substitute any novelty print you may have. Of course, then it won't be an angel ribbon quilt, but it will be beautiful anyway even if it has to be renamed "Rose Ribbons" or "Pussy Cat Ribbons".

**APPROXIMATE SIZE**
50" x 50"

**BLOCK SIZE**
5" x 5" finished

**TECHNIQUES**
Quarter Square Triangles, Working with Directional Prints

**MATERIALS**
1 yard novelty print 1
5/8 yard white fabric
1/4 yard yellow fabric
1/2 yard pink fabric (includes cornerstones)
3/4 yard green fabric (includes first border)
1 yard novelty print 2
1/2 yard binding
3 yards backing
Batting

**CUTTING**
Blocks

32 squares, 6" x 6", novelty print 1
16 squares, 6¼" x 6¼", white (cut in quarters diagonally)
4 squares, 6¼" x 6¼", yellow (cut in quarters diagonally)
7 squares, 6¼" x 6¼", pink (cut in quarters diagonally)
5 squares, 6¼" x 6¼", green (cut in quarters diagonally)

Finishing

5 strips, 2"-wide, green (first border)
6 strips, 4"-wide, novelty print 2 (second border)
4 squares, 4" x 4", pink (cornerstones)
6 strips, 2½"-wide, binding

# INSTRUCTIONS

## Blocks

1. If you are using a directional fabric, you will need to take a little more care in order to make sure that all your blocks face the correct direction. Cut the 6" novelty print 1 squares diagonally in half. Cut 16 going from the lower left to the upper right and 16 going from the upper left to the lower right. (**Diagram 1**) Be sure to keep triangles in four separate stacks. **Note:** *If your novelty print is not directional, you can cut your all your squares diagonally in the same direction.*

### Diagram 1

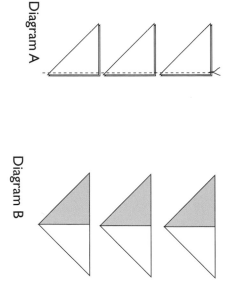

2. Place a white triangle and a yellow triangle right sides together with white triangle on the top; sew together. (**Diagram 2**) You will need 16 white/yellow triangle pairs.

### Diagram 2

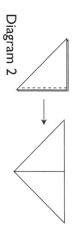

**Hint:** *Chain piecing can speed up the process of sewing several triangles together. Just continue to feed pairs of triangles under the presser foot. Do not clip threads between triangle pairs. (**Diagram A**) When you are done, clip threads and press seams toward the darker triangle. (**Diagram B**)*

### Diagram A

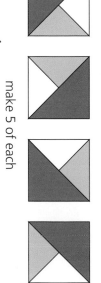

### Diagram B

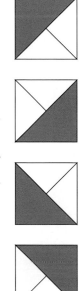

3. Repeat step two with white and pink triangles and the white and green triangles. You will need 28 white/pink triangles pairs and 20 white/green triangle pairs. (**Diagram 3**)

### Diagram 3

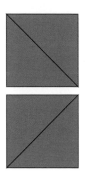

4. Using four novelty print 1 triangles from each stack, sew to white/yellow triangles. (**Diagram 4**)

### Diagram 4

make 4 of each

5. Using seven novelty print 1 triangles from each stack, sew to white/pink triangles. (**Diagram 5**)

### Diagram 5

make 7 of each

6. Using five novelty print triangles from each stack, sew to white/green triangles. (**Diagram 6**)

### Diagram 6

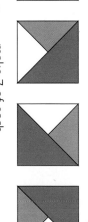

make 5 of each

*Finishing*

**Note:** *Sew quilt together in four sections.*

1. For section 1, place blocks in four rows of four blocks noting positions. Sew together in rows then sew rows together, (**Diagram 7**)

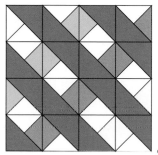

Diagram 7

2. For section 2, place blocks in four rows of four blocks noting positions. Sew together in rows then sew rows together, (**Diagram 8**)

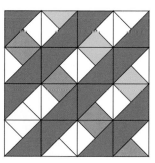

Diagram 8

3. Sew section 1 to section 2. (**Diagram 9**)

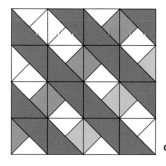

Diagram 9

4. For section 3, place blocks in four rows of four blocks noting positions. Sew together in rows then sew rows together, (**Diagram 10**)

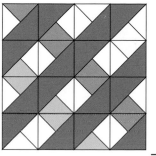

Diagram 10

5. For section 4, place blocks in four rows of four blocks noting positions. Sew together in rows then sew rows together, (**Diagram 11**)

Diagram 11

6. Sew section 3 to section 4. (**Diagram 12**)

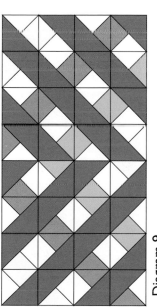

Diagram 12

39

7. Sew all sections together. (Diagram 13)

Diagram 13

8. Measure quilt top lengthwise; sew and cut two 2"-wide pink strips to that length. Sew to sides of quilt. Measure quilt top crosswise; sew and cut two 2"-wide pink strips to that length. Sew to top and bottom of quilt top.

9. Repeat step 8 for second border using 4"-wide novelty print strips.

10. Refer to Finishing, pages 138 to 142, to complete your quilt.

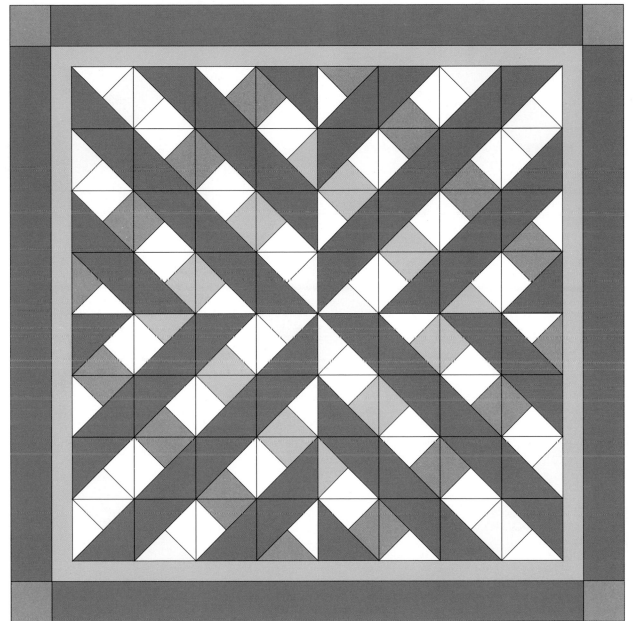

*Angel Ribbons* Quilt Layout

**Time to Finish 22 hours**

# Fairy Godmother

Don't all children need fairy godmothers to keep them safe while they sleep? And what better way to find that fairy than in a novelty print fairy fabric that is then added to this charming quilt.

The lovely fairy print is framed by an intricate looking—but actually simple-to-make—star. When a row of star blocks are sewn together, they actually form a secondary pattern of stars without the fairy grandmother.

If fairies aren't on your list of preferred characters, pick any other print to fill the frames.

Just remember—then there won't be a fairy godmother to accompany the child who receives the quilt as be or she goes off to Dreamland.

## APPROXIMATE SIZE
46" x 56"

## BLOCK SIZE
10" x 10" finished

## TECHNIQUES
Triangle Squares, Stitch and Flip, Working with Directional Prints

## MATERIALS
2 yards novelty print (includes second border)
¾ yard light blue
½ yard medium blue
½ yard blue/green
½ yard binding
3 yards backing
Batting
Fabric marking pencil

## CUTTING
**Note:** If novelty print is directional, see Cutting for Finishing below and cut second border strips first.

### Blocks
12 squares, 6½" x 6½", novelty print
48 squares, 2½" x 2½", light blue
48 squares, 3" x 3", light blue
48 squares, 3" x 3", medium blue
96 squares, 2½" x 2½", blue/green

### Finishing
5 strips, 2½"-wide, blue/green (first border)
*6 strips, 6½"-wide, novelty print (second border)
6 strips, 2½"-wide, binding

*If novelty print is directional, cut two 6½"-wide strips along the crosswise grain, then cut 6½"-wide strips along the lengthwise grain. Measure quilt top when finished to cut exact lengths of strips.

43

# INSTRUCTIONS

*Blocks*

1. Using a fabric marking pencil, draw a diagonal on wrong side of 48 of the 2¹/₂" x 2¹/₂" blue/green squares. (**Diagram 1**)

**Diagram 1**

2. Place a marked 2¹/₂" x 2¹/₂" blue/green square right sides together at one corner of a 6¹/₂" x 6¹/₂" novelty print square. Sew along drawn line. (**Diagram 2**)

**Diagram 2**

3. Trim about ¹/₄" from stitching. (**Diagram 3**)

**Diagram 3**

4. Fold back resulting triangle and press. (**Diagram 4**)

**Diagram 4**

5. Repeat steps 2 to 4 at remaining three corners. (**Diagram 5**) Repeat for eleven more novelty squares.

**Diagram 5**

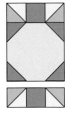

6. Draw a diagonal line on wrong side of 3" x 3" light blue squares. (**Diagram 6**)

**Diagram 6**

7. Place a 3" x 3" light blue square right sides together with a 3" x 3" medium blue square; sew ¹/₄" from each side of drawn line. (**Diagram 7**)

**Diagram 7**

8. Cut along drawn line. (**Diagram 8**)

**Diagram 8**

9. Press open resulting triangle squares. (**Diagram 9**) Repeat with remaining 3" x 3" light blue and medium squares.

**Diagram 9**

10. Trim Triangle Squares to 2¹/₂" if necessary.

11. Sew a Triangle Square to opposite sides of a 2¹/₂" x 2¹/₂" blue/green square. (**Diagram 10**) Repeat three more times.

**Diagram 10**

12. Sew two units from step 11 to opposite sides of 6¹/₂" x 6¹/₂" novelty print square. (**Diagram 11**)

**Diagram 11**

13. Sew 2¹/₂" x 2¹/₂" light blue square to each end of two units from step 11. (**Diagram 12**) Repeat.

**Diagram 12**

14. Sew to top and bottom of block. (**Diagram 13**)

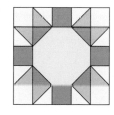

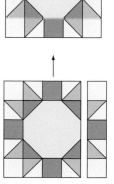

**Diagram 13**

15. Repeat steps 11 to 14 for eleven more blocks.

*Finishing*

1. Place blocks in four rows of three blocks. Sew together in rows then sew rows together.

2. Measure quilt top crosswise; cut two 2¹/₂"-wide blue/green strips to that length. Sew to top and bottom of quilt. Measure quilt lengthwise; cut two 2¹/₂"-wide blue/green strips to that length. Sew to sides of quilt.

3. Repeat step 2 for second border using 6¹/₂"-wide novelty print strips.

4. Refer to Finishing, pages 138 to 142, to complete your quilt.

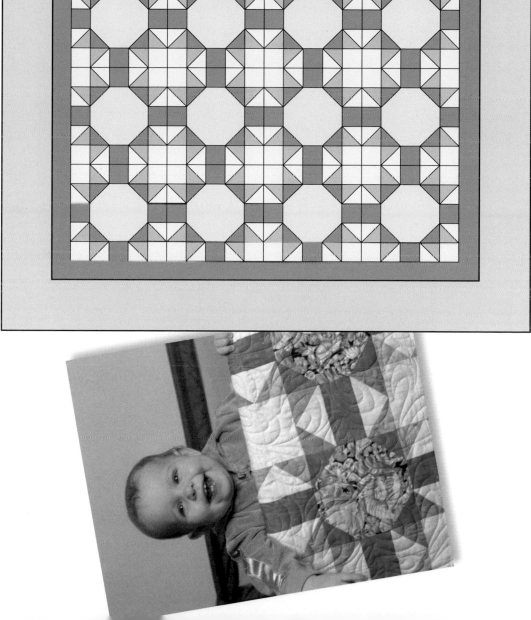

*Fairy Godmother* Quilt Layout

45

# My Paper Dolls

**APPROXIMATE SIZE**
42" x 51"

**BLOCK SIZE**
7½" x 7½" finished

**TECHNIQUES**
Log Cabin-style Piecing or Foundation Piecing (optional), Working with Directional Prints

**MATERIALS**
2 yards novelty print (includes border)
5/8 yard light peach fabric
3/4 yard dark peach fabric
3/4 yard blue fabric (sashing)
1/2 yard binding
2 yards backing
Batting

**PATTERN**
Log Cabin Block (page 51)

**CUTTING**
Blocks
*20 squares, 5½" x 5½", novelty print
20 strips, 1¾" x 5½", light peach
20 strips, 1¾" x 6¾", light peach
20 strips, 1¾" x 6¾", dark peach
20 strips, 1¾" x 8", dark peach

Finishing
25 strips, 1¾" x 8", blue (vertical sashing)
6 strips, 1¾" x 37½", blue (horizontal sashing)
*6 strips, 3½"-wide (border)
6 strips, 2½"-wide, binding

*If you have a directional print, cut the crosswise (top and bottom) borders first. Then cut the side borders vertically.

**Time to Finish**
**12 hours**

Because I loved to play with paper dolls as a child, when I spied this paper doll fabric, I knew I had to make a quilt with that charming fabric.

To show off the print, I wanted to use a simple pattern so I chose to make the quilt using a simplified Log Cabin. It's a great way to frame any novelty print that's just too enchanting to cut up.

Of course, now that I've made the quilt, it's going in my Hope Chest (I'm hoping for a grand-daughter who likes to play with paper dolls).

# INSTRUCTIONS

## Blocks

**Note:** *The blocks in this quilt are simple Log Cabin blocks that can be pieced with or without foundations.*

1. To make blocks without a foundation, sew a $1^3/4$" x $5^1/2$" light peach strip to the right edge of a $5^1/2$" x $5^1/2$" novelty print square. (**Diagram 1**)

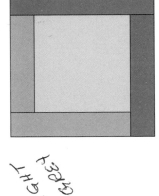

**Diagram 1**

2. Turn the block clockwise and sew $1^3/4$" x $6^3/4$" light peach strip to right edge. (**Diagram 2**)

**Diagram 2**

3. Turn block clockwise again and sew a $1^3/4$" x $6^3/4$" dark peach strip. (**Diagram 3**)

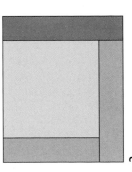

**Diagram 3**

4. Finally, turn and sew $1^3/4$" x 8" dark peach strip to complete block. (**Diagram 4**) Make 20 blocks.

**Diagram 4**

5. To make blocks with a foundation, make 20 foundations using pattern on page 51 and referring to Preparing the Foundation, page 133.

6. Piece 20 blocks referring to How to Make a Foundation-Pieced Block, pages 134 to 138. **Note:** *The finished block will be a mirror image to the pattern.*

48

*Finishing*

1. Place blocks in five rows of four blocks each.

2. Sew blocks together in rows with 1³/₄" x 8" blue sashing strips alternating with blocks. Sew rows together with 1³/₄" x 37¹/₂" blue sashing between rows and at top and bottom. (**Diagram 5**)

3. Measure quilt crosswise; cut the 3¹/₂"-wide crosswise novelty strips to that measurement. Sew to top and bottom of quilt.

4. Measure quilt lengthwise; cut the 3¹/₂"-wide lengthwise novelty print strips to that length. Sew to sides of quilt.

5. Refer to Finishing, pages 138 to 142, to complete your quilt.

**Diagram 5**

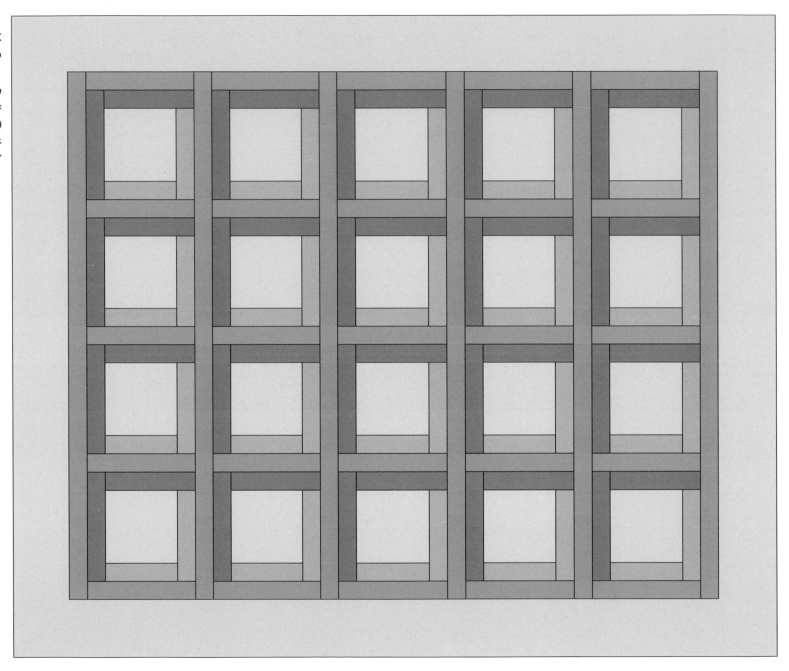

Log Cabin Foundation

C

1

2

3

4

51

*I am an avid baseball fan so, of course, I'd buy any fabric that celebrates my favorite sport. By making the blocks a modified Attic Window, the quilt has the appearance that you are looking outside watching the kids play baseball! The quilt looks complicated, but it is so easy you'll want to make one for each of the players on the team.*

*Another quilt for my Hope Chest (I'm hoping for a grandson who likes to play baseball).*

# Little League

**APPROXIMATE SIZE**
39¹/₂" x 52"

**BLOCK SIZE**
6" x 7" finished

**TECHNIQUES**
Attic Windows, Triangle Squares

**MATERIALS**
1 yard novelty print
¹/₂ yard light brown fabric
¹/₂ yard dark brown fabric
⁵/₈ yard red fabric (sashing)
1¹/₄ yards blue (border, binding)
2 yards backing
Batting

**CUTTING**
Blocks

20 rectangles, 5" x 6", novelty print
20 strips, 2" x 5", light brown
20 strips, 2" x 6", dark brown
10 squares, 2¹/₂" x 2¹/₂", light brown
10 squares, 2¹/₂" x 2¹/₂", dark brown

Finishing

15 strips, 1¹/₂" x 7¹/₂", red (sashing)
4 strips, 1¹/₂" x 27¹/₂", red (sashing)
2 strips, 1¹/₂" x 39¹/₂", red (sashing)
2 strips, 1¹/₂" x 29¹/₂", red (sashing)
6 strips, 4¹/₂"-wide, blue (border)
6 strips, 2¹/₂"-wide, blue (binding)

# INSTRUCTIONS

*Blocks*

1. Sew 2" x 6", dark brown strip to left edge of 5" x 6" novelty print rectangle. (**Diagram 1**)

**Diagram 1**

2. Using a fabric pencil, draw a diagonal line on wrong side of 2 1/2" x 2 1/2" light brown squares. Place light brown and dark brown squares right sides together. Sew 1/4" from each side of drawn line. Cut along drawn line. Fold resulting triangle squares open and press. (**Diagram 2**)

**Diagram 2**

3. Sew a triangle square to 2" x 5" light brown strip noting position of triangle square. (**Diagram 3**)

**Diagram 3**

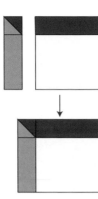

4. Sew to lower edge of novelty print rectangle to complete block. (**Diagram 4**) Make 20 blocks.

**Diagram 4**

*Finishing*

1. Place blocks in five rows of four blocks each.

2. Sew blocks together in rows with 1 1/2" x 7 1/2" red strips in between. Sew rows together with 1 1/2" x 27 1/2" red strips in between rows. (**Diagram 5**)

**Diagram 5**

3. Sew 1 1/2" x 39 1/2" red strips to sides of quilt. Sew 1 1/2" x 29 1/2" red strips to top and bottom. (**Diagram 6**)

**Diagram 6**

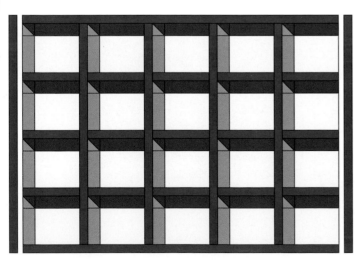

4. Measure quilt lengthwise; cut two 4½"-wide blue strips to that length. Sew to sides of quilt.

5. Measure quilt crosswise; cut two 4½"-wide blue strips to that length. Sew to top and bottom of quilts

6. Refer to Finishing, pages 138 to 142, to complete your quilt.

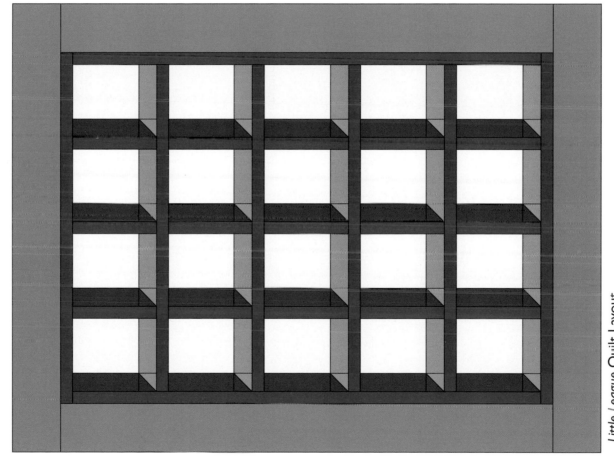

*Little League* Quilt Layout

Time to Finish
13 hours

# Baby's Garden

Little children love flowers and critters. Put them together in a quilt, and every child will be delighted. Our beautiful garden is the home of this clever Baby's Garden quilt. The border floral print was the inspiration for the colors used in the blocks.

This quilt looks very complicated, but by using the Easy Appliqué method described on page 132, this quilt can be finished in less than a day! That will give you plenty of time for the oobing and aabing that is sure to come from all who see this quilt.

**APPROXIMATE SIZE**
43" x 54"

**BLOCK SIZE**
10" x 10" finished

**TECHNIQUE**
Easy Appliqué

**MATERIALS**
1½ yards light blue (background)
scraps yellow, orange, blue, brown, pink, purple, red, light green, medium green, dark green, white
¼ dark green (sashing)
⅛ turquoise (cornerstones)
green floral (border)
½ yard binding
3 yards backing
Batting
Invisible monofilament thread
1 yard lightweight paper-backed fusible web
Permanent black marking pen

**PATTERNS**
Butterfly (page 62)
Sun (page 61)
Bird (page 60)
Flower 1 (page 63)
Flower 2 (page 64)
Turtle (page 67)
Caterpillar (page 65)
Frog (page 66)
Ladybugs (page 64)

**CUTTING**

Blocks

**Note:** Cut out patterns to Appliqué referring to Easy Appliqué, pages 132 to 133.

12 squares, 10½" x 10½", light blue (background)

## Finishing

31 strips, 1³/₄" x 10¹/₂", dark green (sashing)
20 squares, 1³/₄" x 1³/₄", turquoise (cornerstones)
6 strips, 4¹/₂"-wide, green floral (border)
6 strips, 2¹/₂"-wide, binding

## INSTRUCTIONS

### Blocks

1. Referring to Easy Appliqué, pages 132 to 133, to make 12 blocks. Draw details on blocks using a permanent black fabric marker. (**Diagram 1**)

**Diagram 1**

## Finishing

1. Place blocks in four rows of three blocks. Sew blocks together in rows with 1³/₄" x 10¹/₂" dark green strips in between and on each end. Sew four 1³/₄" turquoise cornerstones and three 1³/₄" x 10¹/₂" dark green strips together in rows. (**Diagram 2**)

2. Sew block rows and sashing rows together.

3. Measure quilt lengthwise; cut two 4¹/₂"-wide green floral strips to that length. Sew to sides of quilt. Measure quilt crosswise; cut two 4¹/₂"-wide green floral strips to that length. Sew to top and bottom of quilt.

4. Refer to Finishing, pages 138 to 142, to complete your quilt.

**Diagram 2**

Baby's Garden **Quilt** Layout

Bird Appliqué

Sun Appliqué

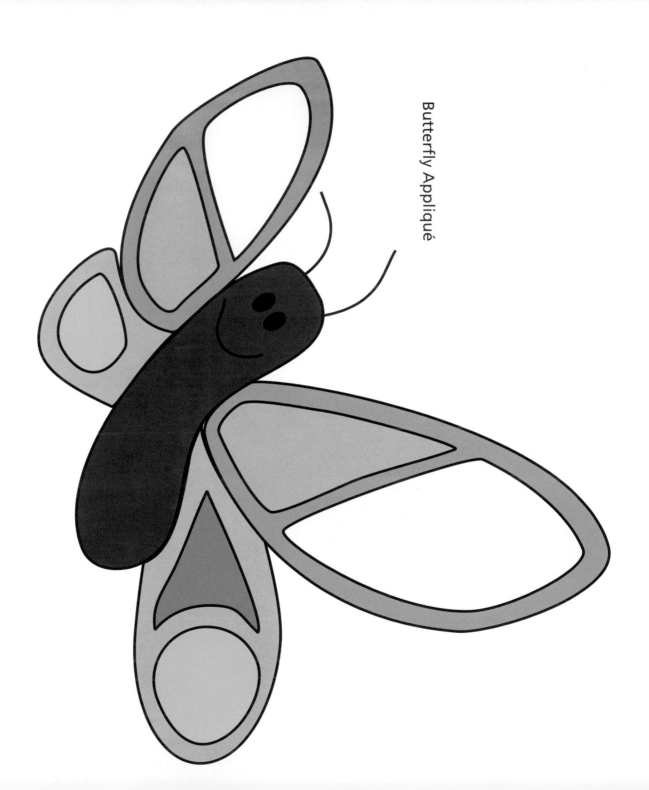

Butterfly Appliqué

Flower 1 Appliqué

Ladybugs Appliqué

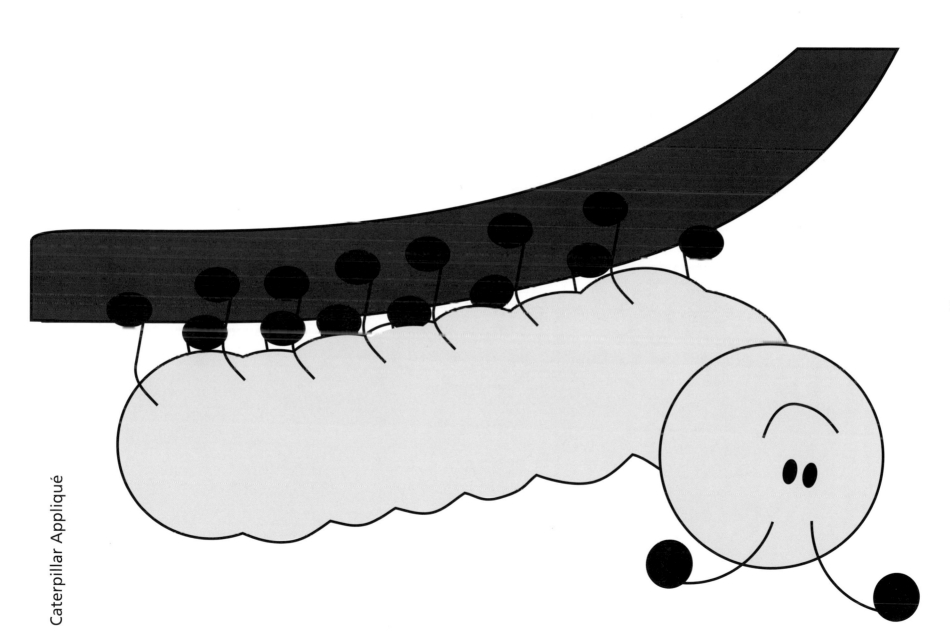

Caterpillar Appliqué

Frog Appliqué

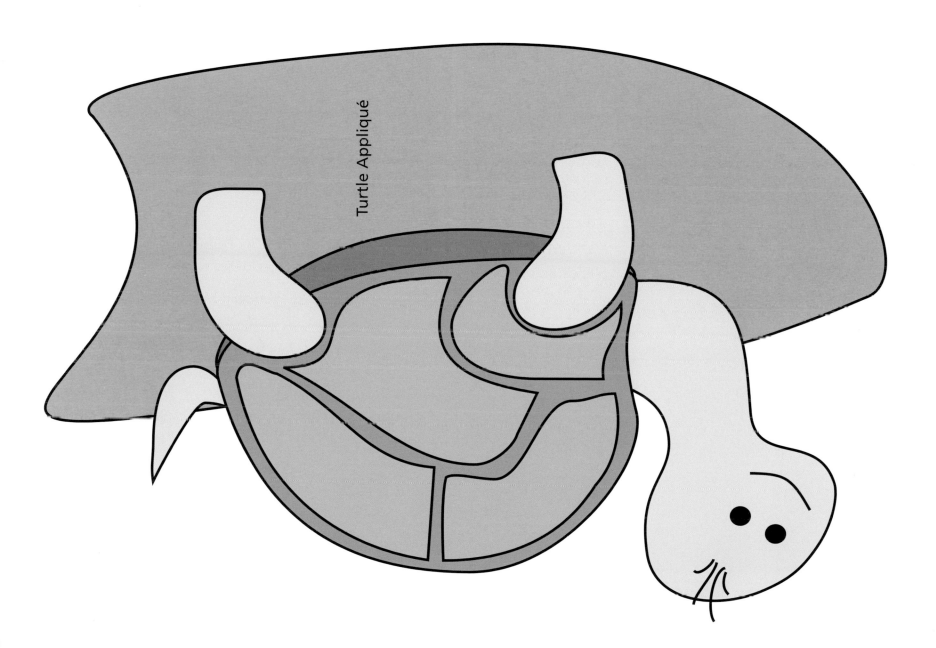

Turtle Appliqué

67

**Time to Finish 23 1/2 hours**

# Lost in the Stars

*Find the stars made from the pink and yellow triangles that dance across this quilt. Inside each star whimsical flowers and animals dance. In fact, some of the flowers and animals seem to enjoy dancing so much they've continued dancing outside the stars.*

*The entire quilt is made with simple-to-make triangle squares and foundation piecing.*

**APPROXIMATE SIZE**
44" x 56"

**BLOCK SIZE**
4" x 4" finished

**TECHNIQUES**
Foundation Piecing and Triangle Squares

**MATERIALS**
1 yard novelty print
3/4 yard pink print
3/4 yard yellow print
1 1/2 yards blue print
3/4 yard yellow print (border)
1/2 yard binding
2 2/3 yards backing
Batting

**PATTERNS**
Blocks A and B (page 71)

**CUTTING**

Blocks

**Note:** *You do not have to cut exact pieces for foundation piecing.*

54 squares, 3 1/4" x 3 1/4", novelty print (Blocks A and 3)
27 squares, 5" x 5", pink print (Triangle Squares)
27 squares, 5" x 5", yellow print (Triangle Squares)
108 strips, 1 3/4" x 3 1/4", blue print (Blocks A and B)
108 strips, 1 3/4" x 4 1/2", blue print (Blocks A and B)

Finishing

6 strips, 4 1/2"-wide, yellow print (border)
6 strips, 2 1/2"-wide, binding

# INSTRUCTIONS

## Blocks

1. For Blocks A and B, make 30 foundations for A and 24 for B referring to Preparing the Foundation, page 133.

2. Make Blocks A and B referring to Making a Foundation-Pieced Block, pages 134 to 138. (**Diagram 1**)

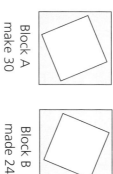

Block A
make 30

Block B
made 24

**Diagram 1**

3. For triangle squares, draw a diagonal line on wrong side of 5" x 5" yellow print squares. Place yellow print square and pink print square right sides together. Sew 1/4" from each side of drawn line. Cut along drawn line. Press resulting triangle squares open. (**Diagram 2**) Repeat with remaining yellow print and pink print square for a total of 54 triangle squares.

make 54

**Diagram 2**

## Finishing

1. Place Blocks A and B and triangle squares in sections of nine. (**Diagram 3**) Note positions of triangle squares.

**Diagram 3**

2. Sew each section in rows then sew rows together.

3. Measure quilt lengthwise; cut two 4¹/2"-wide yellow print strips to that length. Sew strips to sides of quilt. Measure quilt crosswise; cut two 4¹/2"-wide yellow print strips to that length. Sew strips to top and bottom of quilt.

4. Refer to Finishing, pages 138 to 142, to complete your quilt.

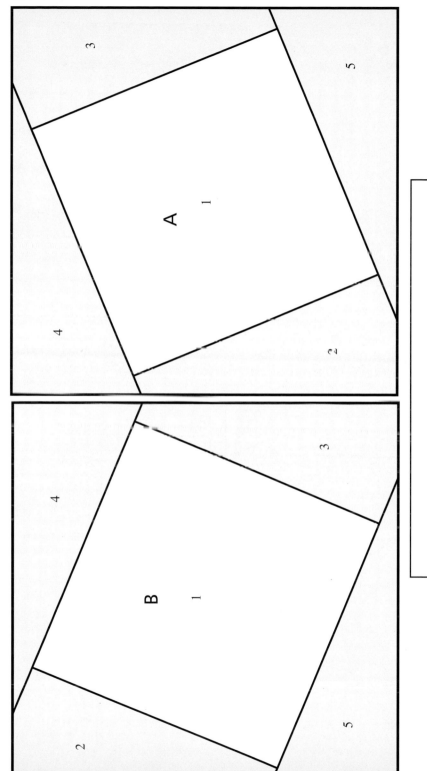

Lost in the Stars Quilt Layout

71

*Oh, yum yum! Licorice, gum-drops, gumballs, lollipops, gummy worms, jelly beans.*

*The sticky problem in making this quilt will be to find all of the various candy prints. Then, by putting them together in the triangle squares called for in the instructions, the candies become pinwheels to add even more excitement to the quilt.*

*What child doesn't love candy! Now every child can have it all without fear of tummy aches or trips to the dentist because the candies are sewn together in a quilt. Who wouldn't think that was fun!*

# Candy Pinwheels

**APPROXIMATE SIZE**
48" x 60"

**BLOCK SIZE**
3" x 3" finished

**TECHNIQUE**
Triangle Squares

**MATERIALS**
1 yard white
½ yard print 1 (licorice print)
½ yard print 2 (gumdrop print)
¾ yard print 3 (gumballs print)
½ yard print 4 (lollipop print)
½ yard print 5 (gummy worm print, includes first border)
1 yard print 6 (jelly bean print, second border)
½ yard binding
3 yards backing
Batting

**CUTTING**
**Triangle Squares**
60 squares, 4" x 4", white
28 squares, 4" x 4", print 1
28 squares, 4" x 4", print 2
40 squares, 4" x 4", print 3
24 squares, 4" x 4", print 4
12 squares, 4" x 4", print 5

**Finishing**
5 strips, 2½"-wide, print 5 (first border)
6 strips, 4½"-wide, print 6 (second border)
6 strips, 2½"-wide, binding

# INSTRUCTIONS

*Triangle Squares*

1. For triangle squares, draw a line on wrong side of the lighter square of a pair of squares. (**Diagram 1**)

**Diagram 1**

2. Place a pair of squares right sides together. Sew 1/4" from each side of drawn line. (**Diagram 2**)

**Diagram 2**

3. Cut along drawn line. Press resulting triangle squares open. (**Diagram 3**)

**Diagram 3**

4. Make 48 A triangle squares from white and print 1; 40 B triangle squares from white and print 3; 40 C triangle squares from prints 2 and 3; 24 D triangle squares from white and print 4; 24 E triangle squares from prints 4 and 5; 8 F triangle squares from white and print 2; and 8 G triangle squares from prints 1 and 2. (**Diagram 4**)

**Diagram 4**

A -make 48    B -make 40    C -make 40

D -make 24    E -make 24    F -make 8

G -make 8

*Finishing*

1. To simplify piecing, place triangle squares in sections of 16 (four across by four down). There are six different sections. (**Diagram 5**)

**Diagram 5**

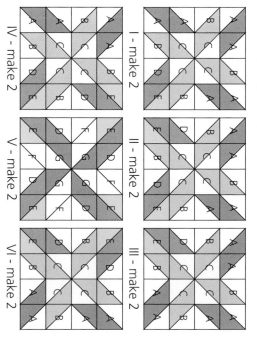

I - make 2    II - make 2    III - make 2

IV - make 2    V - make 2    VI - make 2

2. Sew each section together in rows then sew rows together. Make two of each section.

3. Place sections in four rows of three sections.
(**Diagram 6**)

**Diagram 6**

4. Sew sections together in rows then sew rows together.

5. Measure quilt lengthwise; cut two 2$^1$/2"-wide print 5 strips to that length. Sew to sides of quilt. Measure quilt crosswise; cut two 2$^1$/2"-wide print 5 strips to that length. Sew to top and bottom of quilt.

6. Repeat step 5 for second border using 4$^1$/2"-wide print 6 strips.

7. Refer to Finishing, pages 138 to 142, to complete your quilt.

*Candy Pinwheels* Quilt Layout

# My Baby Genius

*Benartex Fabric has produced Baby Genius, a line of fabric covered with swirls, wiggles, dots and happy faces to tickle a baby's imagination. I bought several fabrics from this line including a panel with assorted picture squares and geometric squares.*

*I decided to break up the geometric squares to add interest and color so I cut those squares into quarters and sewed sashing between the sections. The sashing is a row of the faces which is also a print of one of the large squares.*

*Whether it's going to turn a baby into a genius or not, the fabric has helped to create a fun quilt!*

### APPROXIMATE SIZE
49½" x 59½"

### BLOCK SIZE
9½" x 9½" finished

### TECHNIQUE
Using Novelty Fabric

### MATERIALS
1 yard novelty print (need enough fabric for ten 8" squares and ten 7½" squares)

¼ yard face print
¾ yard blue print
¾ yard green print
¾ yard blue star print
½ yard binding
3 yards backing
Batting

### CUTTING

Block A

10 squares, 8" x 8", novelty print
20 strips, 1½" x 8", blue print
20 strips, 1½" x 10", blue print

Block B

10 squares, 7½" x 7½", novelty print (cut into 4 equal sections, 3¾" x 3¾")
20 strips, 1½" x 3¾", face print
10 strips, 1½" x 8", face print
20 strips, 1½" x 8", blue print
20 strips, 1½" x 10", blue print

Finishing

25 strips, 1½" x 10", green print (sashing)
6 strips, 1½" x 43½", green print (sashing)
7 strips, 3½"-wide, blue star print (border)
7 strips, 2½"-wide, binding

# INSTRUCTIONS

## Block A - *Picture Blocks*

1. Sew 1¹/2" x 8" blue print strips to opposite sides of 8" x 8" novelty print square. (**Diagram 1**) Press seams toward strips.

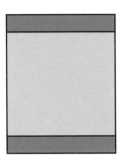

**Diagram 1**

2. Sew 1¹/2" x 10" blue print strips to top and bottom. (**Diagam 2**) Press seams toward strip.

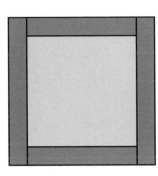

**Diagram 2**          Picture Blocks

3. Repeat steps for ten Block A.

## Block B - *Geometric Blocks*

1. Cut a 7¹/2" x 7¹/2" novelty print square in four equal squares, each 3³/4" x 3³/4".

2. Sew a 3³/4" x 3³/4" square to each side of a 1¹/2" x 3³/4" face print strip. (**Diagram 3**) Repeat.

**Diagram 3**

3. Sew pair of squares to each side of a 1¹/2" x 8" face print strip. (**Diagram 4**)

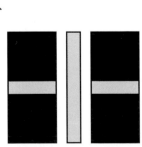

**Diagram 4**

4. Sew 1¹/2" x 8" blue print strips to opposite sides of block. (**Diagram 5**)

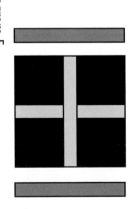

**Diagram 5**

5. Sew 1¹/2" x 10" blue print strips to top and bottom to complete block. (**Diagram 6**) Repeat steps for ten Block B.

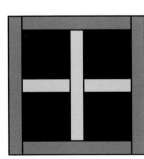

**Diagram 6**          Geometric Blocks

78

*Finishing*

1. Referring to the quilt layout, place blocks in five rows of four blocks each.

2. Sew blocks in rows with $1^{1}/2$" x 10" green print strips in between and at each end. (**Diagram 7**)

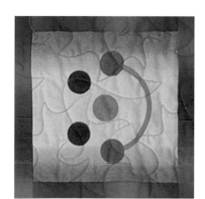

4. Measure quilt top lengthwise; cut two $3^{1}/2$"-wide blue star strips to that length. Sew to sides of quilt. Measure quilt crosswise; cut two $3^{1}/2$"-wide blue star strips to that length. Sew to top and bottom.

5. Refer to Finishing, pages 138 to 142, to complete your quilt.

*My Baby Genius* Quilt Layout

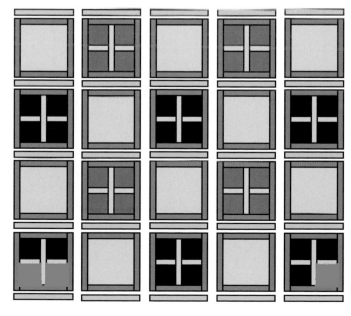

Diagram 7

3. Sew rows together with $1^{1}/2$" x $43^{1}/2$" green strips in between and at top and bottom. (**Diagram 8**)

Diagram 8

79

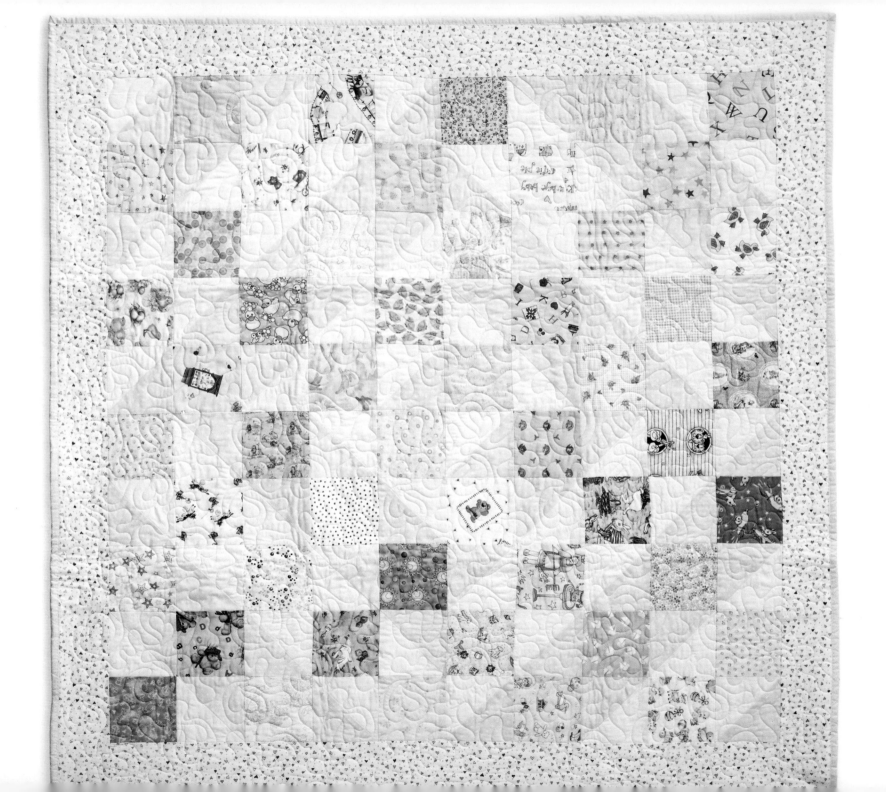

Time to Finish
8 hours

*I purchased a package of 50 squares of baby prints planning to use a few in various quilts. When I spread the fabric out, however, the fabrics seemed to put themselves together into the perfect baby quilt. I decided to use them all, adding a few yards of yellow and white fabric for triangle squares in between the prints plus a matching white print for the border. The design is elegant in its simplicity.*

# Baby Prints

**APPROXIMATE SIZE**
52" x 52"

**BLOCK SIZE**
4¹/₂" x 4¹/₂" finished

**TECHNIQUE**
Triangle Squares

**MATERIALS**
* 1¹/₂ yards total assorted baby prints (enough for fifty 5" squares)
³/₄ yard yellow fabric
³/₄ yard white fabric
1 yard white heart print (border)
¹/₂ yard binding
3¹/₄ yards backing
Fabric marking pencil
Batting

**CUTTING**
Blocks

50 squares, 5" x 5", assorted baby prints
25 squares, 5¹/₂" x 5¹/₂", yellow
25 squares, 5¹/₂" x 5¹/₂", white

Finishing

6 strips, 4"-wide, white heart print (border)
6 strips, 2¹/₂"-wide, binding

# INSTRUCTIONS

## Blocks

1. Using a fabric marking pencil, draw a diagonal line on wrong side of 5¹/₂" x 5¹/₂" white squares. (**Diagram 1**)

**Diagram 1**

2. Place a yellow and white 5¹/₂" x 5¹/₂" square right sides together. Sew ¹/₄" from each side of drawn line. (**Diagram 2**)

**Diagram 2**

3. Cut along drawn line. (**Diagram 3**)

**Diagram 3**

4. Press open resulting triangle squares. (**Diagram 4**) Repeat for all white and yellow 5¹/₂" x 5¹/₂" squares. Trim to 5" square if necessary.

**Diagram 4**

### Finishing

1. Sew quilt top together in sections containing a combination of 25 baby print squares and triangle squares. For Section 1, start with 5" baby print squares and continue to alternate with yellow/white triangle squares in five rows of five blocks. (**Diagram 5**) Sew together in rows then sew rows together. Repeat for another Section 1.

**Diagram 5**

Section 1

2. For Section 2, start with a yellow/white triangle square and continue to alternate with 5" baby print squares in five rows of five blocks. (**Diagram 6**) Sew together in rows then sew rows together. Repeat for another Section 2.

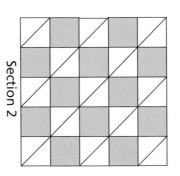

**Diagram 6**

Section 2

3. Sew a section 1 and 2 together for half of the quilt top. Repeat. (**Diagram 7**)

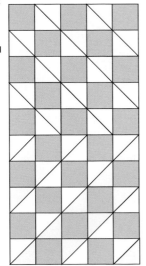

**Diagram 7**

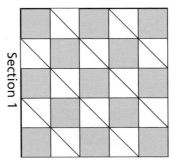

4. Turn one of the halves upside down so quilt top will form a diamond shape and sew together. (**Diagram 8**)

5. Measure quilt top lengthwise; cut two 4"-wide white heart print strips to that length. Sew to sides of quilt top. Measure quilt top crosswise; cut two 4"-wide white heart print strips to that length. Sew to top and bottom of quilt.

6. Refer to Finishing, pages 138 to 142, to complete your quilt.

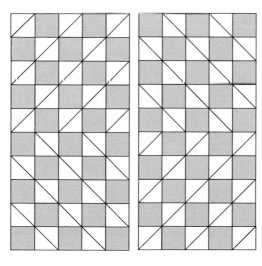

Diagram 8

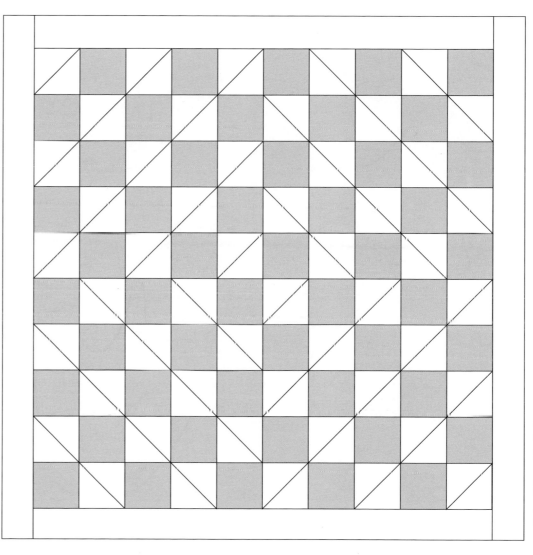

*Baby Prints* Quilt Layout

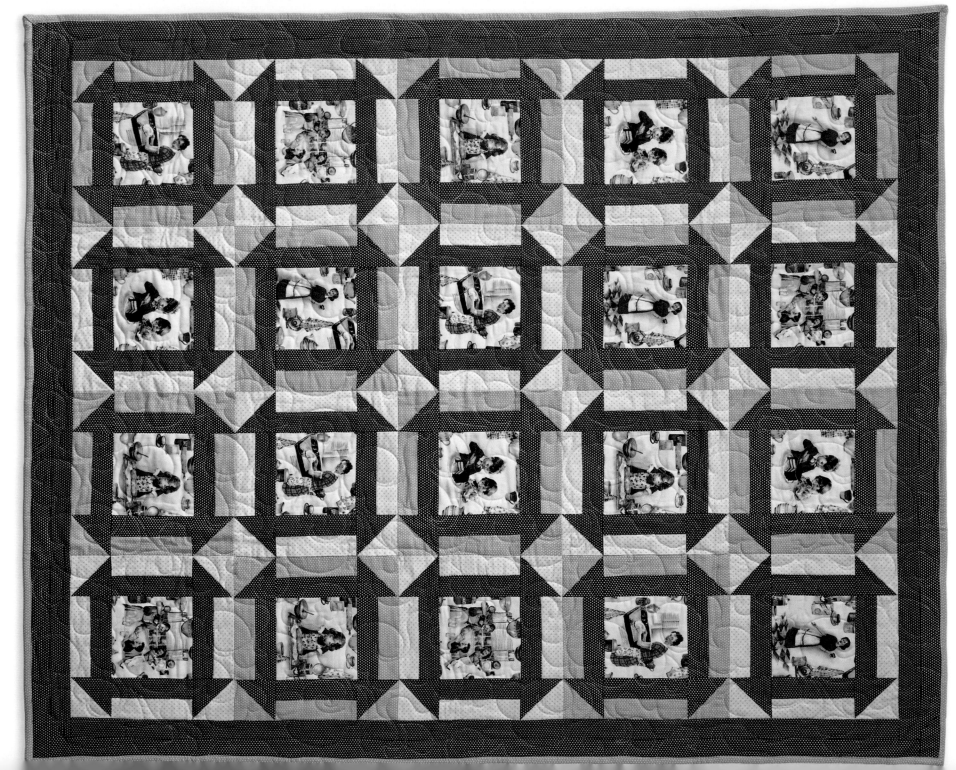

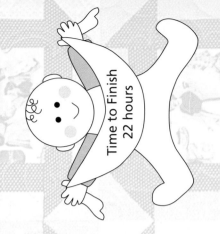

*When I saw this fabric, I knew I had to have it because it reminded me of baking cookies with my mother when I was growing up.*

*The block is actually a modified Churn Dash block. Somehow that seemed to remind me of an old-fashioned butter churn, which would have been used in baking although I never had to use one.*

# Baking Cookies

## APPROXIMATE SIZE
45" x 55"

## BLOCK SIZE
10" x 10" finished

## TECHNIQUES
Triangle Squares, Strip Piecing

## MATERIALS
1 yard novelty print (enough for twenty 5$\frac{1}{2}$" x 5$\frac{1}{2}$" squares)
1 yard blue dot print (includes borders)
1 yard red dot print (includes borders)
1 yard cream dot print
1 yard tan dot print
$\frac{1}{2}$ yard binding
2$\frac{3}{4}$ yards backing
Batting
Fabric marking pencil

## CUTTING
### Blocks
20 squares, 5$\frac{1}{2}$" x 5$\frac{1}{2}$", novelty print
7 strips each, 1$\frac{3}{4}$"-wide, blue dot print and red dot print
7 strips each, 1$\frac{3}{4}$"-wide, cream dot print and tan dot print
20 squares each, 3$\frac{1}{2}$" x 3$\frac{1}{2}$", blue dot print and red dot print
20 squares each, 3$\frac{1}{2}$" x 3$\frac{1}{2}$", cream dot print and tan dot print

### Finishing
6 strips, 1$\frac{3}{4}$"-wide, red dot print (border)
6 strips, 1$\frac{3}{4}$"-wide, blue dot print (border)
6 strips, 1$\frac{3}{4}$"-wide, binding

# INSTRUCTIONS

*Blocks*

1. Using a fabric marking pencil, draw a diagonal line on wrong side of 3¹/₂" x 3¹/₂" cream dot print squares. Place cream dot print and red dot print squares right sides together. (**Diagram 1**)

2. Sew ¹/₄" from each side of drawn line. (**Diagram 2**)

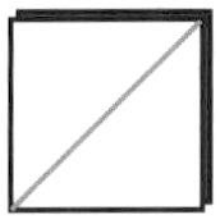

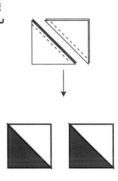

**Diagram 1**      **Diagram 2**

3. Cut along drawn line. Press open resulting triangle squares. (**Diagram 3**) Repeat for all cream and red dot print squares. You will need 40 triangle squares.

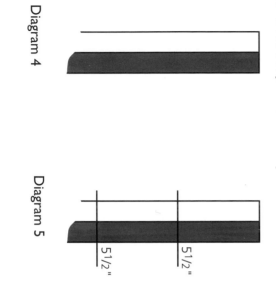

**Diagram 3**

4. Sew 1³/₄"-wide cream and red dot print strips right sides together. Press seams to one side. (**Diagram 4**)

5. Cut strips at 5¹/₂" intervals. (**Diagram 5**) You will need 40 red dot print/cream strips.

**Diagram 4**

5¹/₂"   5¹/₂"

**Diagram 5**

6. Sew strips to opposite sides of 5¹/₂" x 5¹/₂" novelty print squares with red dot print strip next to novelty print square. (**Diagram 6**)

**Diagram 6**

7. Sew a triangle square to each end of a 5¹/₂" strip. Repeat. (**Diagram 7**)

**Diagram 7**

8. Sew to top and bottom to complete block. (**Diagram 8**) Repeat steps 7 to 9 for ten red/cream dot blocks.

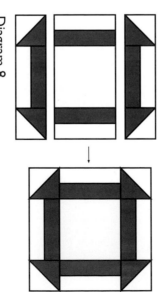

**Diagram 8**

9. Repeat steps 1 to 9 for ten blue/tan dot blocks. (**Diagram 9**)

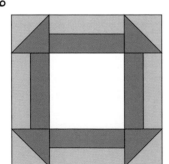

**Diagram 9**

## Finishing

1. Place blocks in five rows of four blocks, alternating red and blue blocks. Sew blocks together in rows then sew rows together.

2. Measure quilt lengthwise; piece and cut two $1^3/4"$-wide red dot print border strips to that length. Sew to sides of quilt. Measure quilt crosswise; piece and cut two $1^3/4"$-wide red dot border strips to that length. Sew to top and bottom of quilt top.

3. Repeat step 2 with $1^3/4"$-wide blue dot print border strips.

4. Refer to Finishing, pages 138 to 142, to complete your quilt.

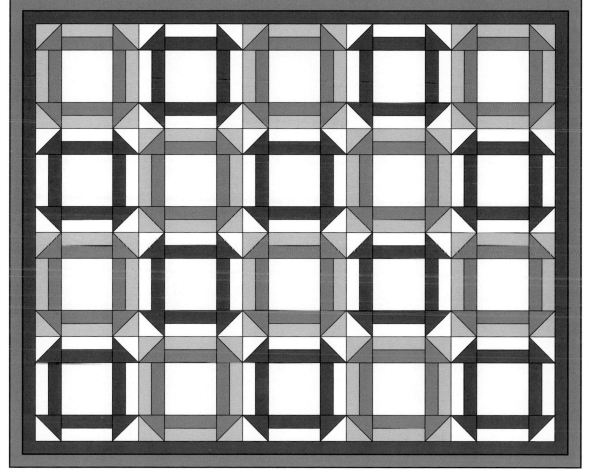

*Baking Cookies* Quilt Layout

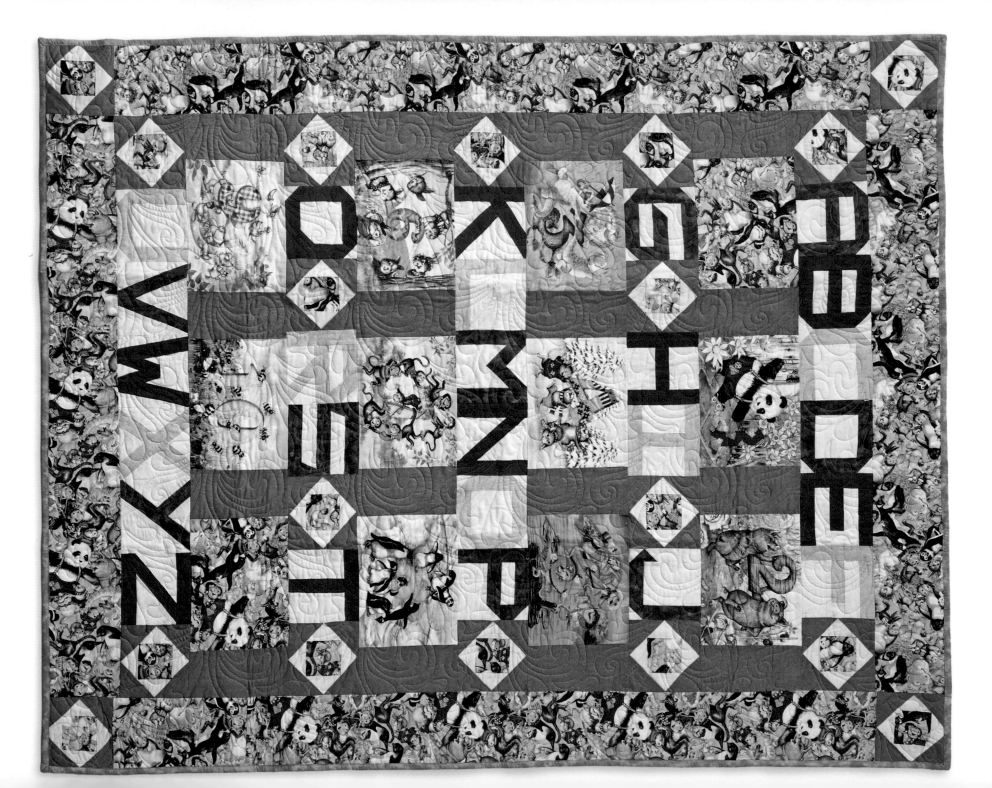

Time to Finish
20 hours

# Now I Know My Numbers and ABCs

I found a fabric panel with the numbers 1 to 10 that was supposed to be made into a fabric book teaching a child about numbers. I loved the fabric, and it gave me the idea to make a quilt that would teach both numbers and ABCs.

Because I'm not sure if you'll be able to find the same fabric, I've given you appliqué patterns for the numbers. In order to finish the quilt quickly, you'll want to use the Easy Appliqué method described on page 132. The alphabet blocks are quickly made with foundation piecing.

What a delightful way to teach your favorite child his numbers and his ABCs!

## APPROXIMATE SIZE
50" x 65"

## BLOCK SIZE
Alphabet blocks, 5" x 5" finished
Square in a Square blocks, 5" x 5" finished
Number blocks, 9" x 7" finished

## TECHNIQUES
Foundation Piecing, Easy Appliqué (optional)

## MATERIALS
1 yard *novelty print 1 (large print for Number blocks)
2 yards novelty print 2 (small print for Square in a Square blocks and border)
1/2 yard yellow fabric
1/2 yard red fabric
1/2 yard blue fabric
1 yard light green fabric
1/2 yard dark green fabric
1/2 binding
3 yards backing
Batting
1/2 yard lightweight paper-backed fusible web

*The novelty print 1 fabric used for this quilt was intended to be a children's fabric book of numbers 1 through 10. If you cannot find fabric with numbers, patterns for Easy Appliqué are given on pages 107 to 111. If you use the Easy Appliqué method, you will need 3/4 yard of a background fabric and 1/4 yard of a contrasting fabric for the numbers.

## PATTERNS
Alphabet Foundations (pages 93 to 105)
Square in a Square Foundation (page 106)
Number Appliqués (pages 107 to 111)

## CUTTING
**Note:** You do not have to cut exact pieces for foundation piecing.

Blocks

12 rectangles, 9 1/2" x 7 1/2", novelty print 1 (Number blocks)
18 squares, 3" x 3", novelty print 2 (Square in a Square blocks)
6 to 7 strips, 1 3/4"-wide, light green (Square in a Square blocks)
36 squares (cut in half diagonally), 3 1/2" x 3 1/2", dark green (Square in a Square blocks)

Finishing
16 rectangles, 3³/₄" x 7¹/₂", dark green (sashing)
6 strips, 5¹/₂"-wide, novelty print 2 (border)
6 strips, 2¹/₂"-wide, binding

# INSTRUCTIONS

*Foundation Blocks*

1. Referring to Foundation Piecing, pages 133-138, make a foundation for each letter of the Alphabet using patterns on pages 93 to 105. Make 18 foundations for Square in a Square blocks using pattern on page 106.

2. Make blocks referring to photograph and layout. (Diagram 1)

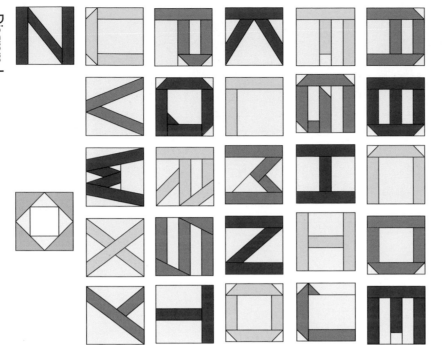

Diagram 1

*Appliqué Blocks*

**Note:** *If you find fabric with numbers, you can eliminate this step.*

1. Refer to Easy Appliqué, pages 132 to 133, to appliqué numbers on 9¹/₂" x 7¹/₂" novelty print 1 rectangles. You will have two rectangles left over. (Diagram 2)

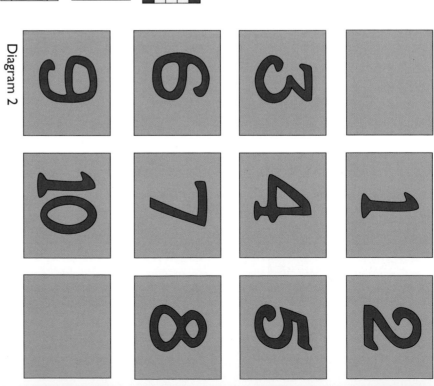

Diagram 2

*Finishing*

1. Rows 1, 3, 5, 7, and 9 are the Alphabet rows. Place Alphabet blocks and Square in a Square blocks according to **Diagram 3**. Sew blocks together in rows.

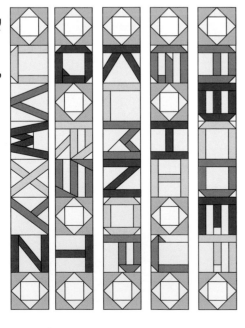

Diagram 3

2. Rows 2, 4, 6, and 8 are the Number blocks. Place Number blocks alternating the 3¾" x 7½" dark green rectangles referring to **Diagram 4**. Sew the blocks together in rows.

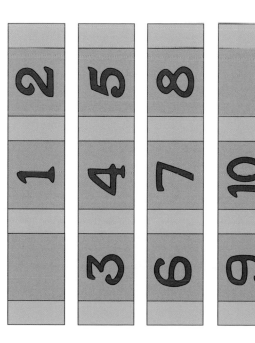

**Diagram 4**

3. Sew rows together. (Diagram 5)

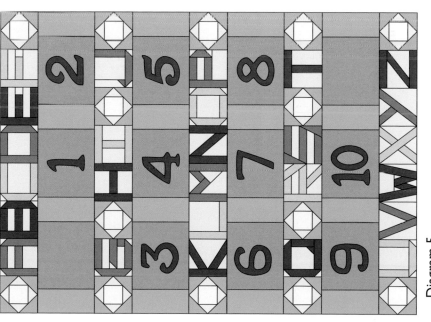

**Diagram 5**

4. Measure quilt lengthwise and crosswise. Cut two 5½"-wide novelty print 2 strips the lengthwise measurement and two 5½"-wide novelty print 2 strips the crosswise measurement. Sew lengthwise strips to the sides of the quilt top. Sew a Square in a Square block to each end of crosswise strips. Sew to top and bottom of quilt top. (**Diagram 6**)

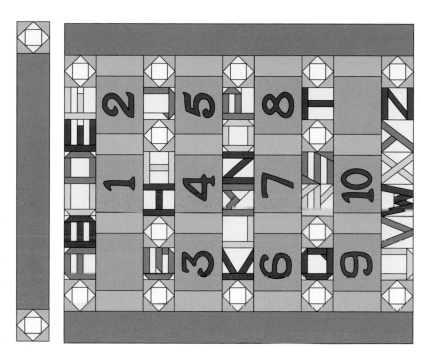

Diagram 6

5. Refer to Finishing, pages 138 to 142, to complete your quilt.

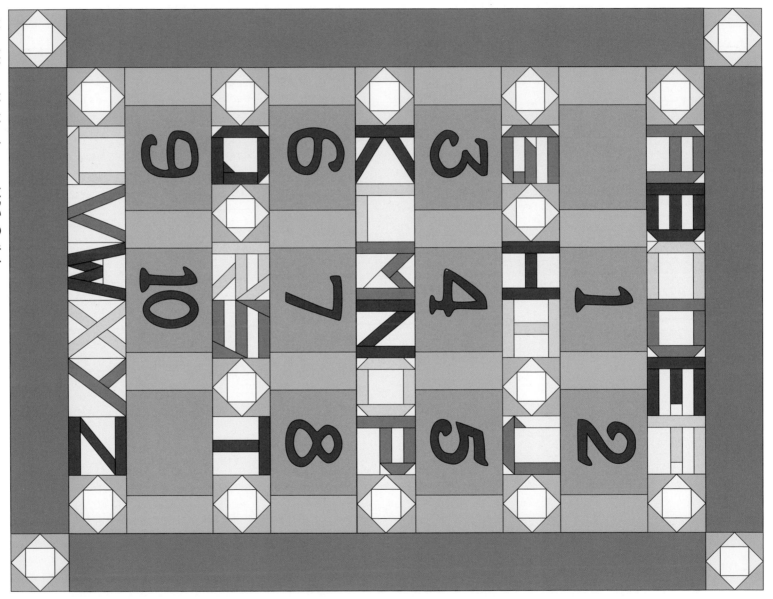

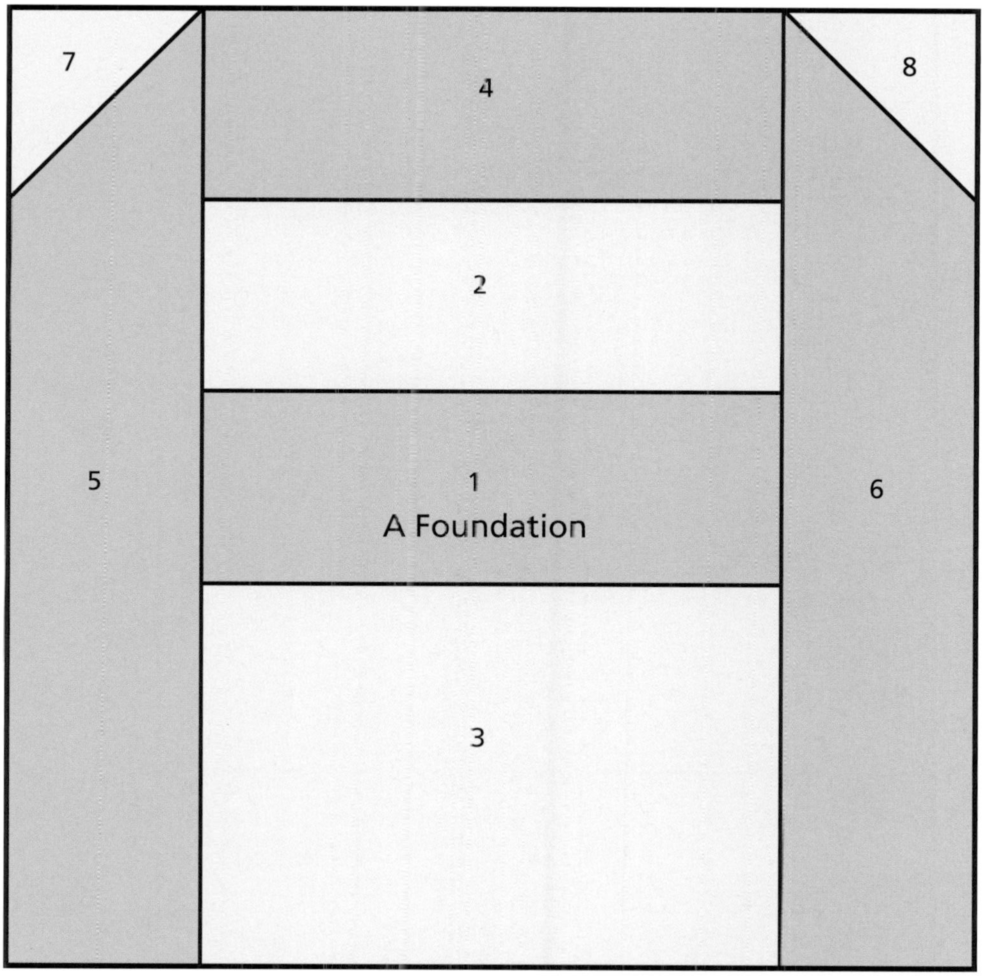

**A Foundation**

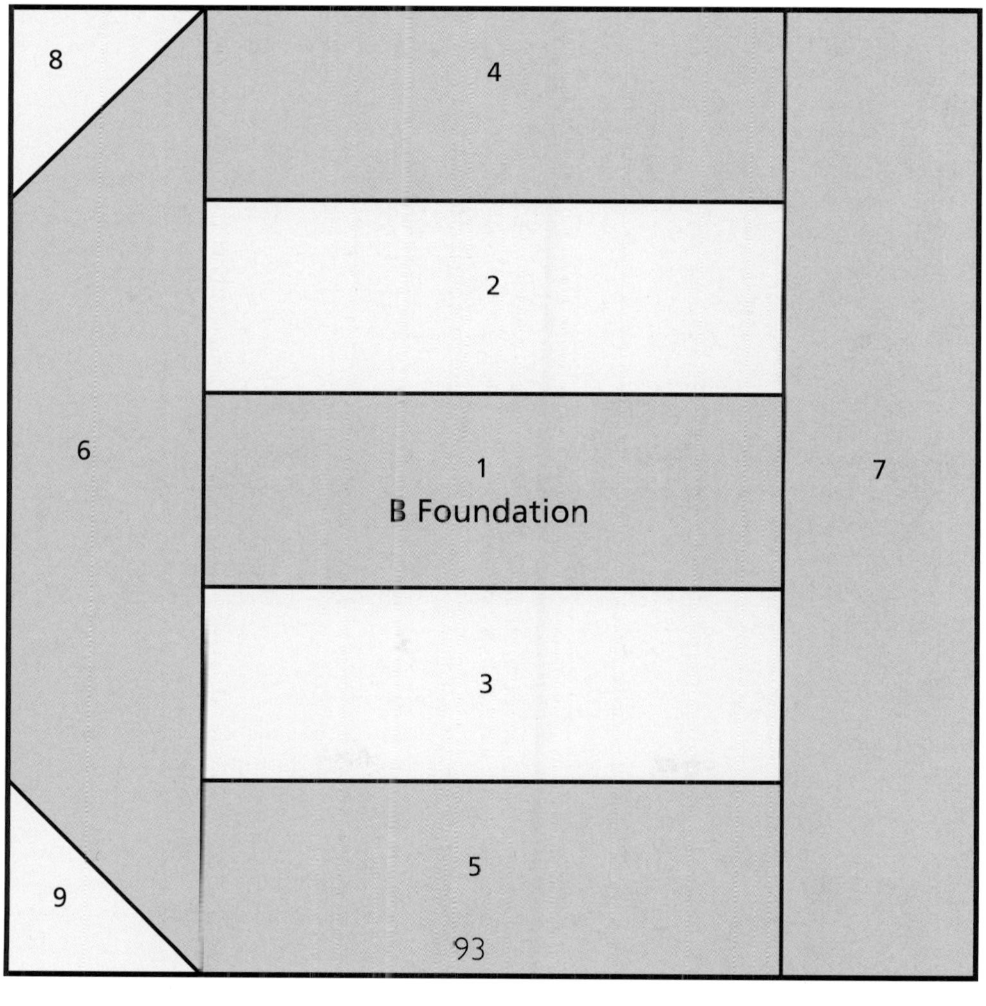

8

6

4

2

1

3

7

5

**B Foundation**

8

7

4

2

1

3

5

93

6

9

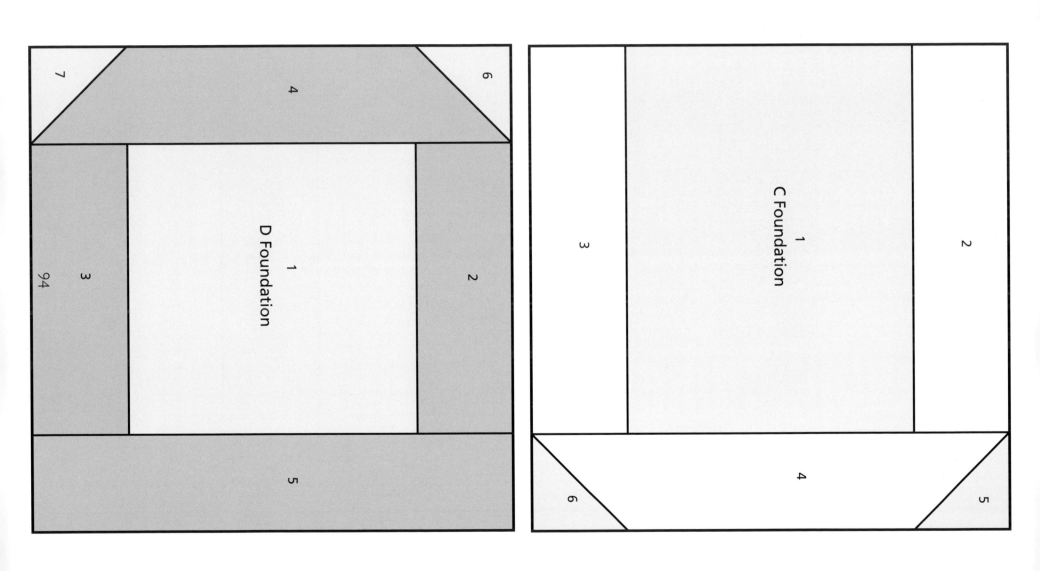

E Foundation

F Foundation

95

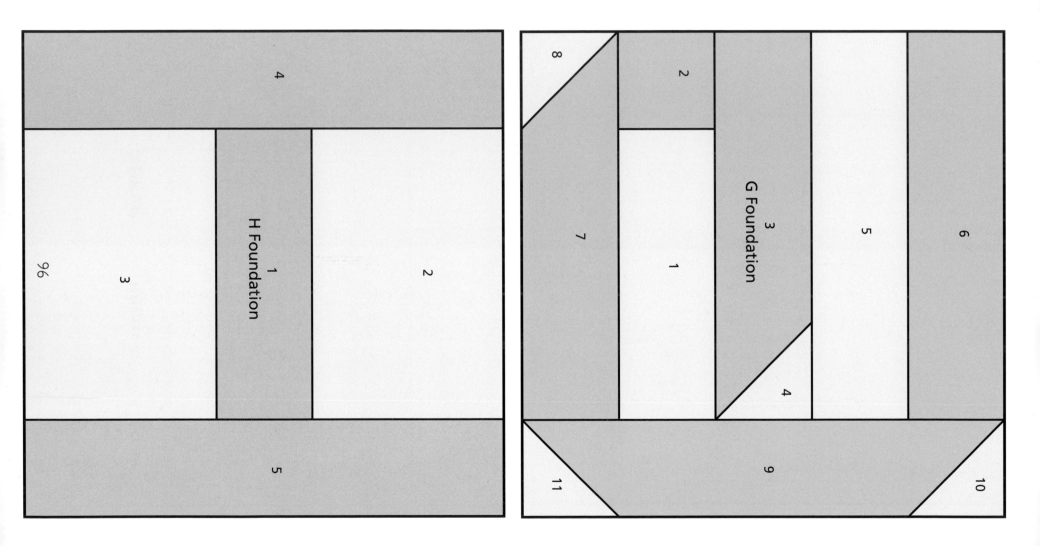

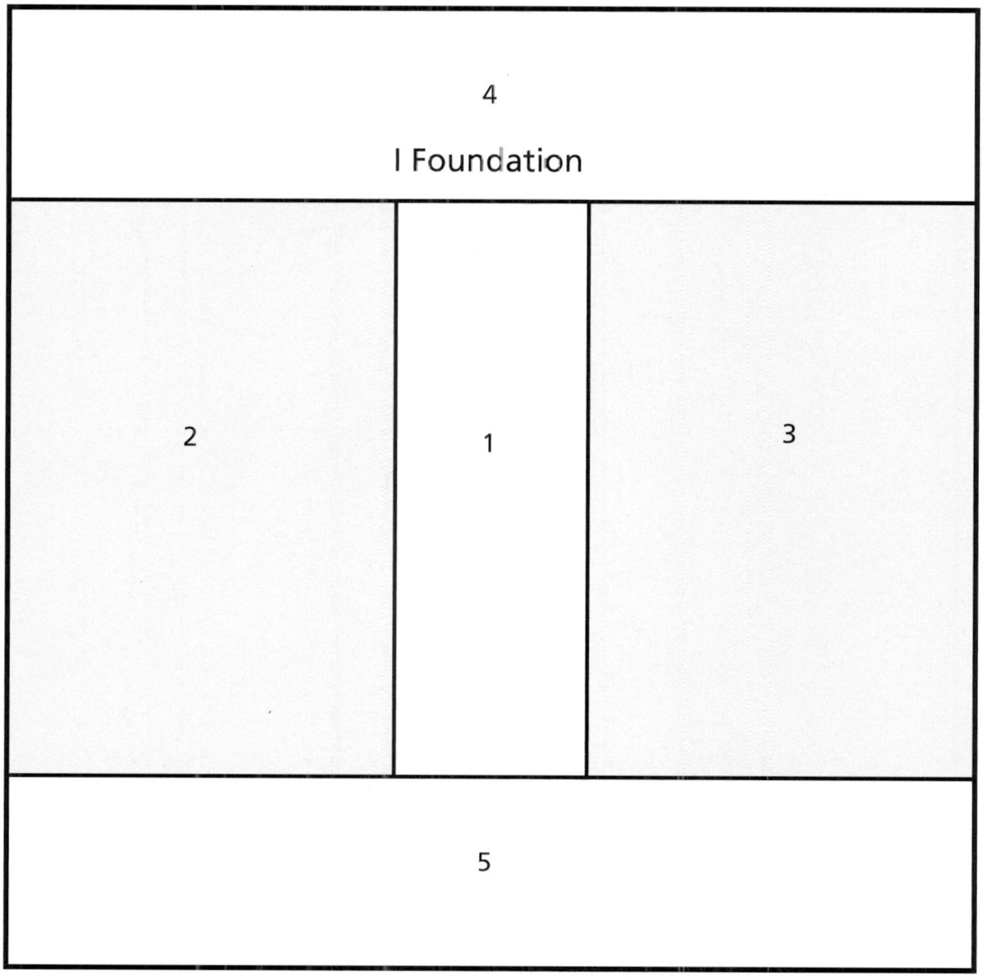

I Foundation

4

3

1

2

5

J Foundation

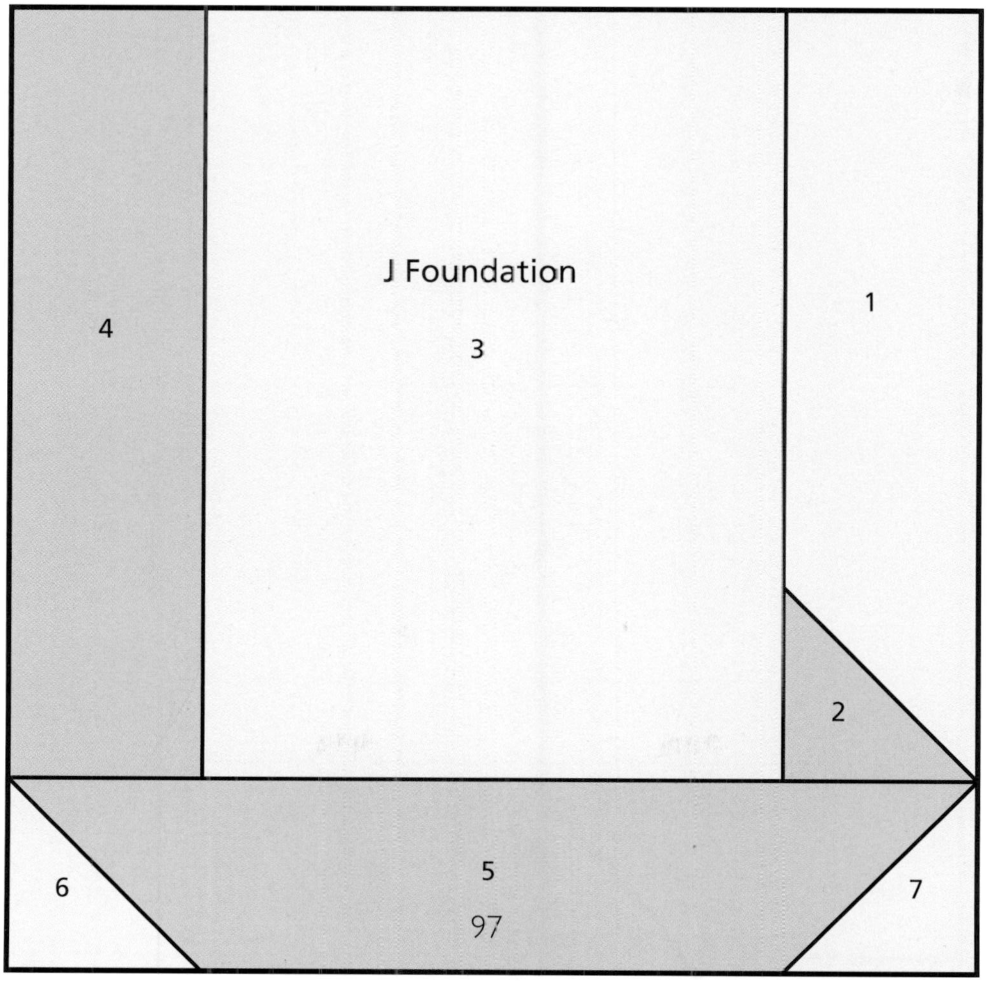

1

2

7

3

4

5

97

6

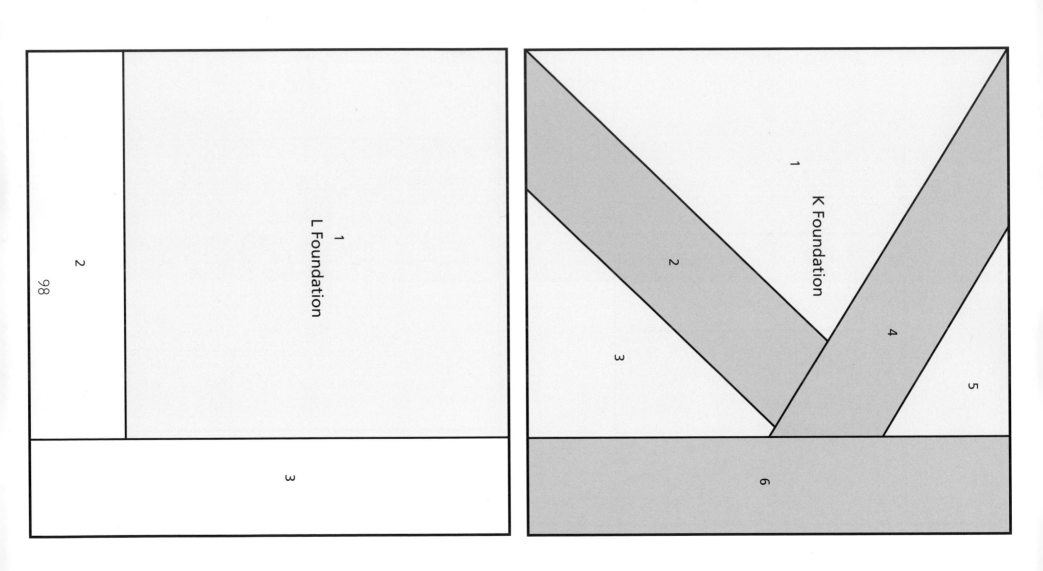

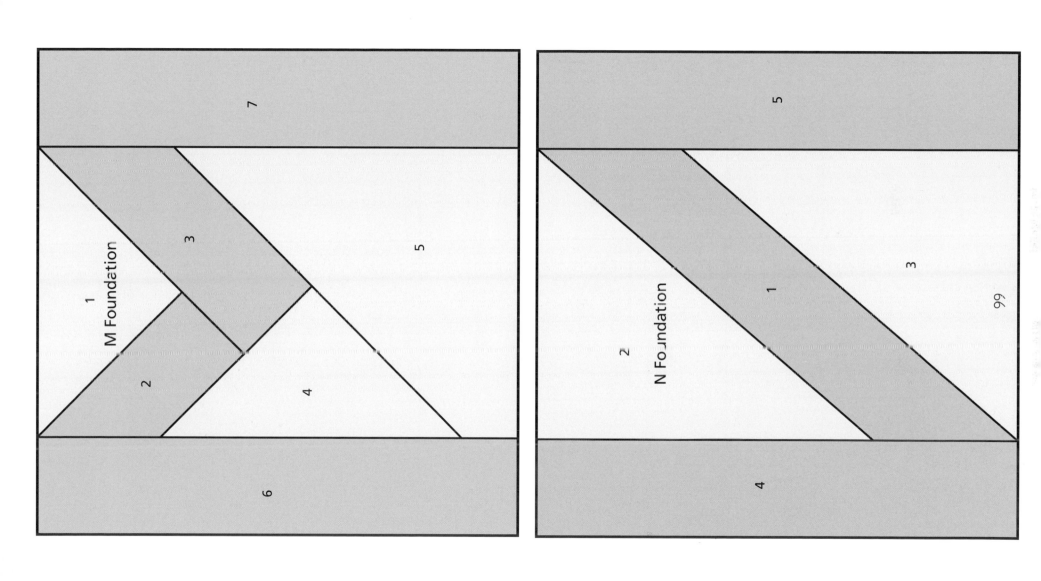

M Foundation

1

2

3

4

5

6

7

N Foundation

1

2

3

4

5

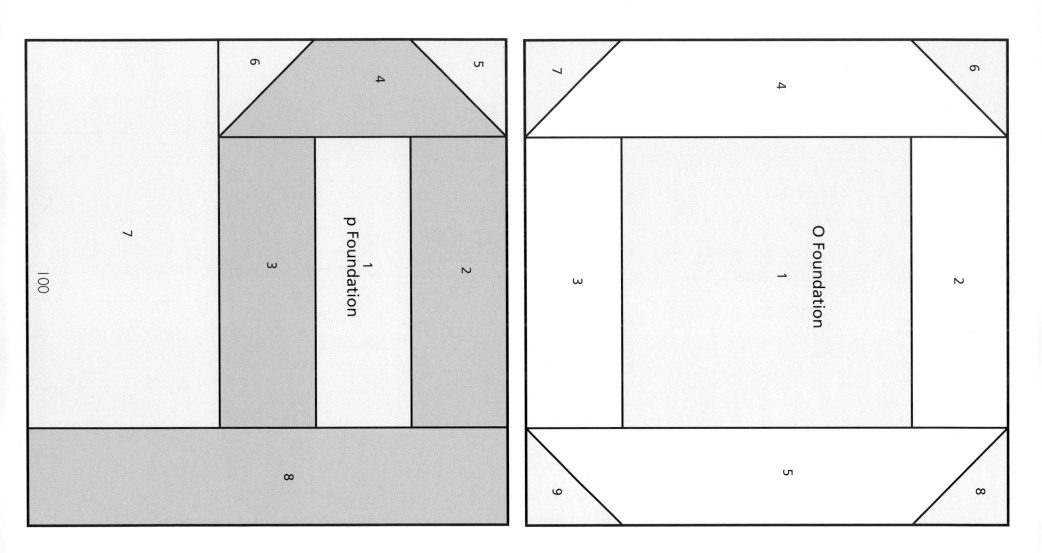

100

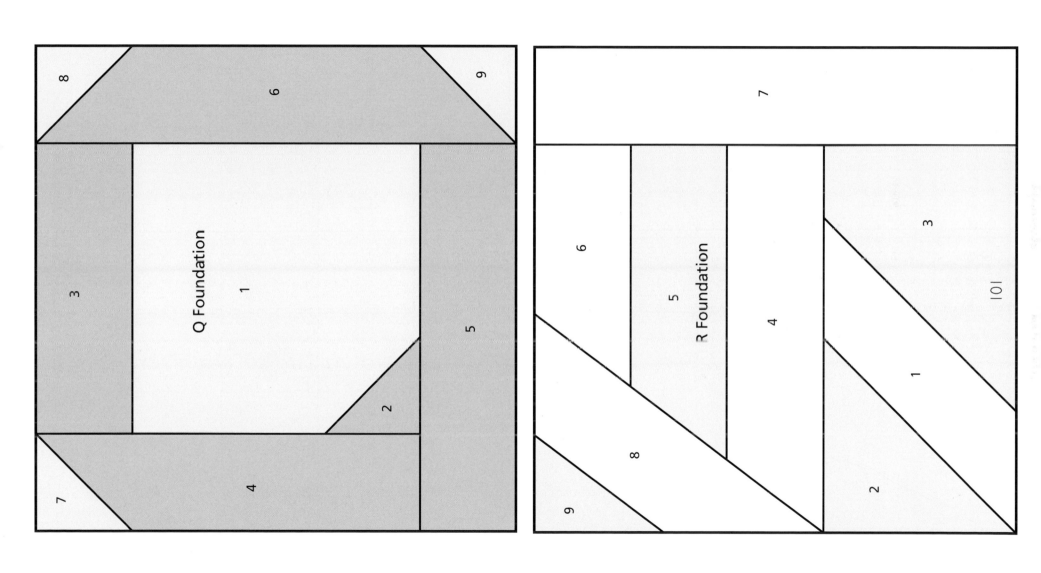

Q Foundation

1

2

3

4

5

6

7

8

9

R Foundation

1

2

3

4

5

6

7

8

9

101

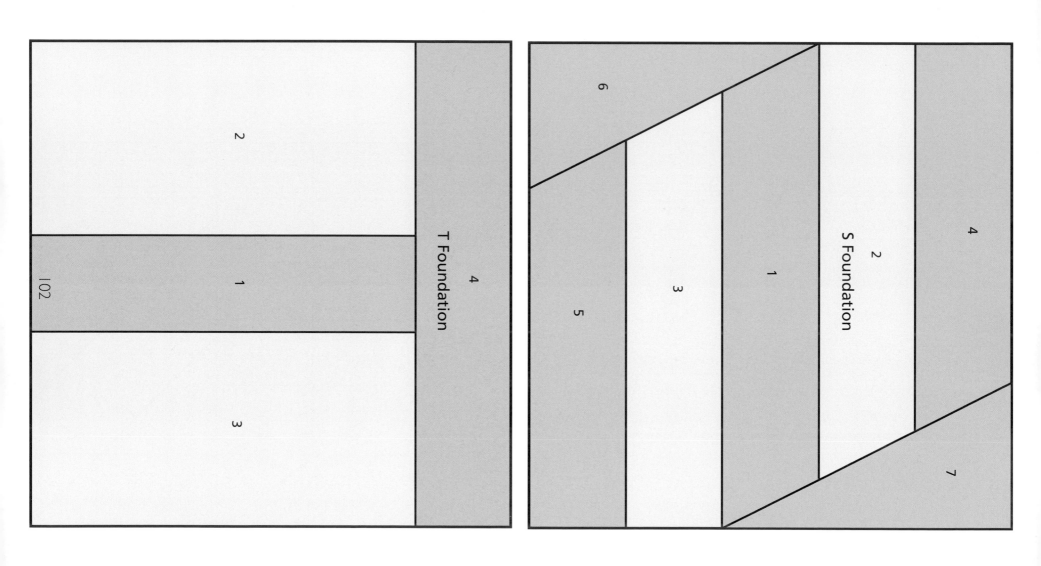

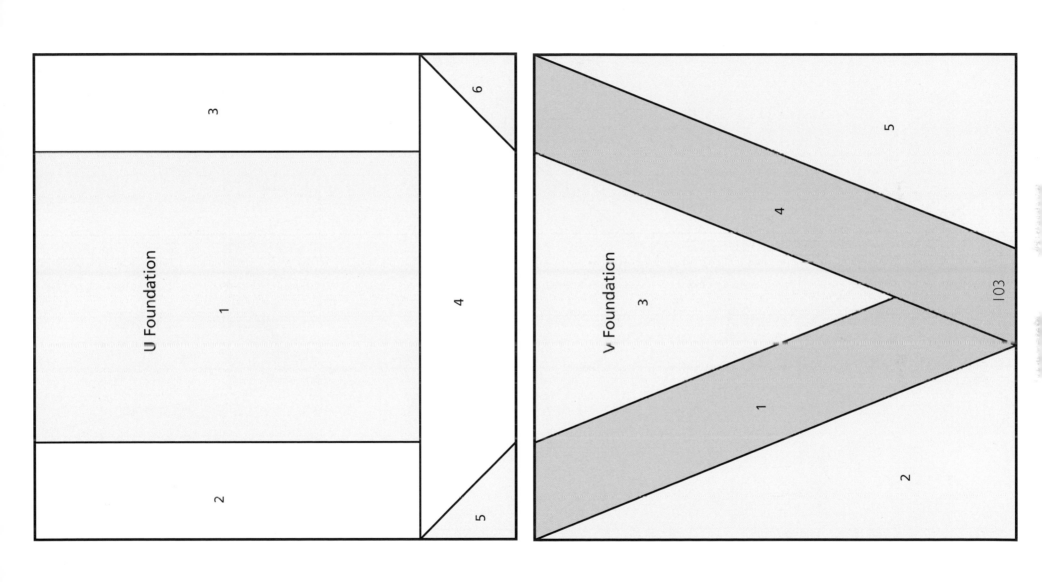

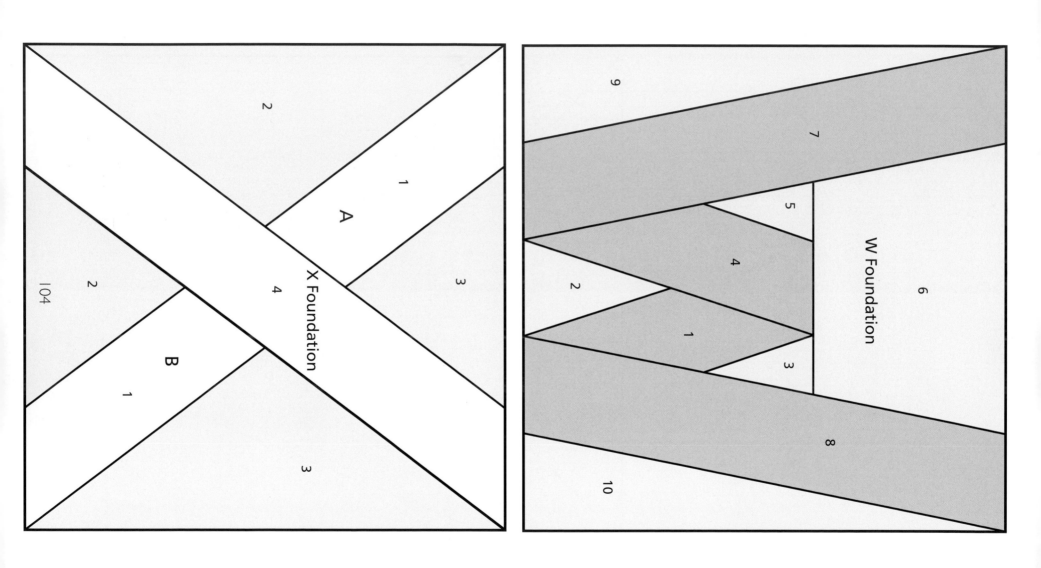

X Foundation

A 1

2

3

4

104

2

B 1

3

W Foundation

9

7

5

4

2

1

3

6

8

10

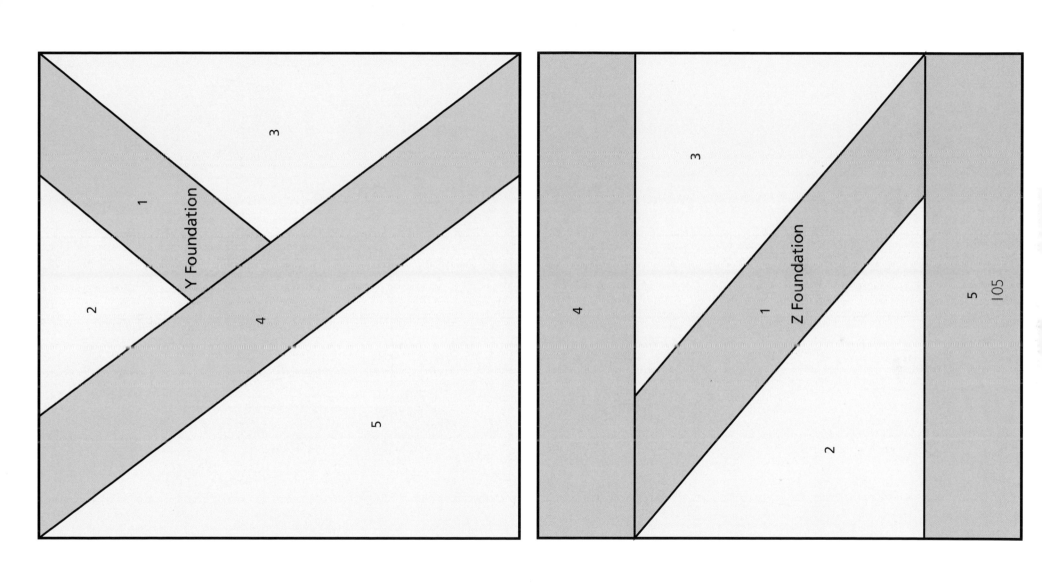

Y Foundation

Z Foundation

105

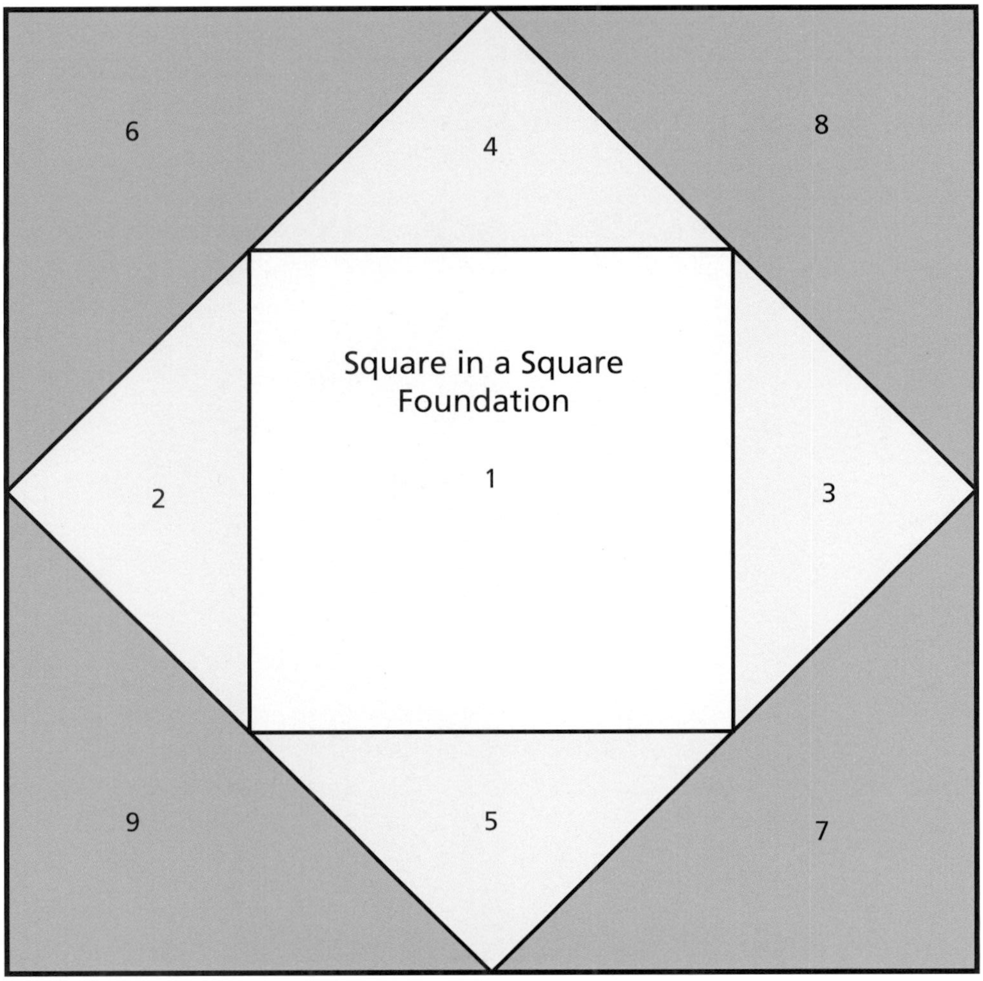

Square in a Square
Foundation

1

2

3

4

5

6

7

8

9

Appliqué Patterns
for 1 anc 2

Appliqué Patterns
for 5 and 6

Appliqué Patterns
for 7 and 8

Appliqué Patterns for
9 and 0 (10)

# Baby's Favorite Things

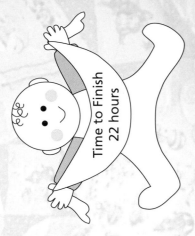

Time to Finish
22 hours

**APPROXIMATE SIZE**
44" x 54"

**BLOCK SIZE**
Star blocks, 5" x 5" finished

**TECHNIQUE**
Foundation Piecing

**MATERIALS**
1 yard novelty print 1 (alternating squares)
1 yard novelty print 2 (block centers)
1 yard novelty print 3 (second border)
1 yard light pink
1 yard dark pink print (includes first border)
1 yard white print
½ yard binding
2½ yards backing
Batting

**PATTERNS**
Star Block A, B, C (page 115)

**CUTTING**
Star Blocks

**Note:** *You do not need to cut exact pieces for foundation piecing, but you may use the following guidelines to piece your Star Blocks.*

32 squares, 2¾" x 2¾", novelty print 2
128 squares, 1⅞" x 1⅞", light pink
64 rectangles, 2¼" x 3⅝", white print (cut diagonally in half)
64 rectangles, 2¼" x 3⅝", dark pink print (cut diagonally in half)

Plain Squares

31 squares, 5½" x 5½", novelty print 1

Finishing

6 strips, 1½"-wide, dark pink print
6 strips, 4"-wide, novelty print 3
6 strips, 2½"-wide, binding

What an easy quilt to make.
Just follow these five simple rules:

*1. Find a novelty print fabric with darling babies; find other fabrics with baby's toys.*

*2. Cut thirty-one 5½" squares from one of the novelty prints.*

*3. Using the Foundation Piecing method described on page 133, make 32 Star blocks.*

*4. Sew the blocks together alternating the plain squares and the foundation-pieced squares.*

*5. Add the borders, and following the instructions on pages 138 to 142, finish the quilt.*

*Now stand back and get the kisses from an adorable baby who just loves her new quilt. Wasn't that a quick and easy way to be the "Favorite" of a darling baby?*

# INSTRUCTIONS

## Star Blocks

1. Refer to Preparing the Foundation, page 133, and make foundations for 32 Star Blocks A, B and C. **(Diagram 1)**

**Diagram 1**

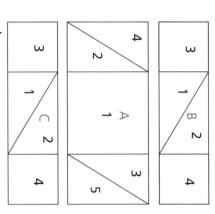

2. Make A, B, and C sections referring to Making a Foundation-pieced Block, pages 134 to 138. Sew sections together to complete Star block. **(Diagram 2)** Make 32 Star blocks.

**Diagram 2**

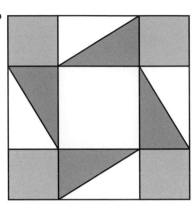

## Finishing

1. Place Star blocks and plain Squares alternating in nine rows of seven. **(Diagram 3)**

2. Sew blocks together in rows then sew rows together.

3. Measure quilt top lengthwise; sew and cut two 1¹/₂"-wide dark pink print strips to that length. Sew to sides of quilt. Measure quilt crosswise; sew and cut two 1¹/₂"-wide dark pink print strips. Sew to top and bottom of quilt.

4. Repeat step 3 for second border using 4"-wide novelty print 3 strips.

5. Refer to Finishing, pages 138 to 142, to complete your quilt.

**Diagram 3**

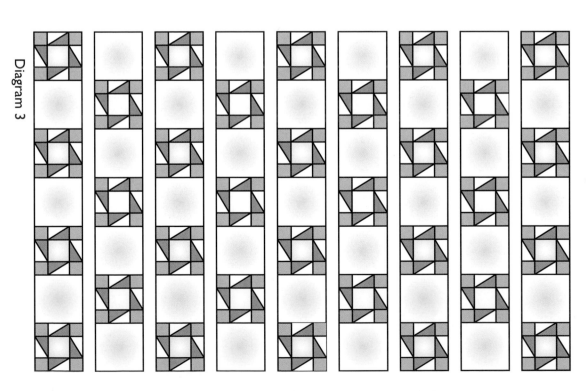

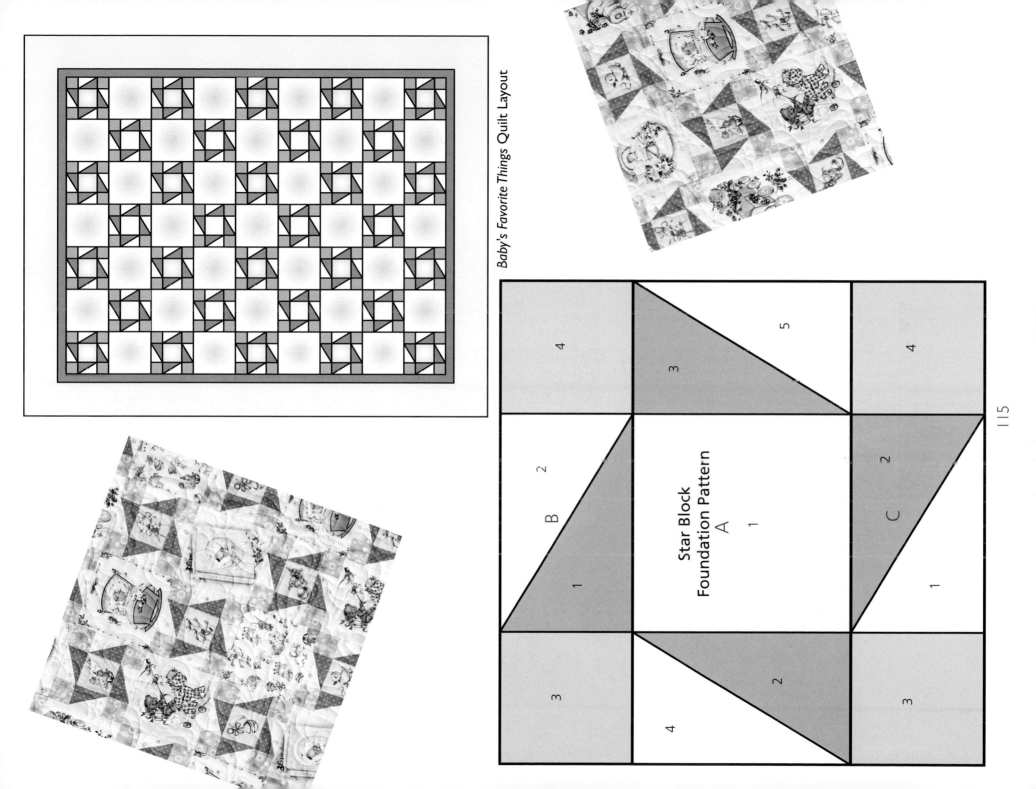

Baby's *Favorite Things* Quilt Layout

Star Block
Foundation Pattern

115

# Baby's Crazy Quilt

**APPROXIMATE SIZE**
37 1/2" x 40 1/2"

**BLOCK SIZE**
Crazy Quilt blocks, 3 1/2" x 3 1/2" finished

**TECHNIQUE**
Foundation Piecing

**MATERIALS**
1 yard novelty print (alternating rectangles)
Fat quarters blue print, pink, green print, cream/pink floral
1 yard pink (sashing)
1/2 yard blue floral (border)
1/2 yard binding
2 1/2 yards backing
Batting

**PATTERNS**
Crazy Quilt Block (page 119)

**CUTTING**
Crazy Quilt Blocks
**Note:** You do not need to cut exact pieces for foundation piecing.

Novelty Rectangles
9 rectangles, 6" x 7", novelty print

Finishing
12 rectangles, 6" x 4", pink (horizontal sashing)
12 rectangles, 4" x 7", pink (vertical sashing)
4 strips, 4"-wide, blue floral (border)
4 strips, 2 1/2"-wide, binding

*For some reason, this old-fashioned novelty print, which I love, made me think of a crazy quilt. I wasn't too sure that a crazy quilt would make a good choice for a baby quilt, but the crazy quilt idea kept repeating itself to me.*

*Then I hit upon the idea of using the novelty print for the rectangular blocks and adding crazy quilt blocks which would be cornerstones with a solid sashing. It was fun to find fat-quarter prints for the crazy blocks that matched the old-fashioned novelty print. To make things really easy, the crazy quilt blocks are made by the foundation-piecing method.*

*Now baby can have a crazy quilt too.*

# INSTRUCTIONS

## Crazy Quilt Blocks

1. Refer to Preparing the Foundation, page 133, and make foundations for 20 Crazy Quilt Blocks. (Diagram 1)

**Diagram 1**

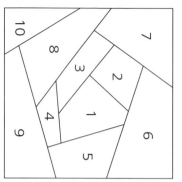

2. Refer to Making a Foundation-pieced Block, pages 134 to 138, to make 20 Crazy Quilt blocks. (Diagram 2).

**Diagram 2**

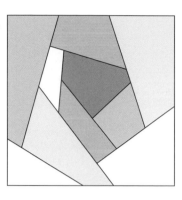

## Finishing

1. For rows 1, 3, 5, and 7, place Crazy Quilt blocks alternating with horizontal sashing strips. For rows 2, 4, and 6, place novelty rectangles, alternating with pink vertical sashing strips. (Diagram 3)

**Diagram 3**

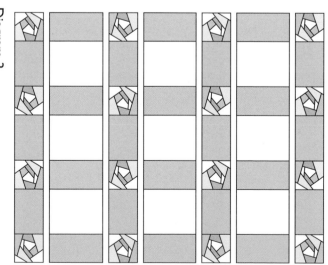

2. Sew blocks, sashing and rectangles together in rows then sew rows together.

3. Measure quilt top lengthwise; cut two 4"-wide blue floral strips to that length. Measure quilt crosswise; cut two 4"-wide blue floral strips to that length. Sew the lengthwise strips to sides of quilt. (Diagram 4)

**Diagram 4**

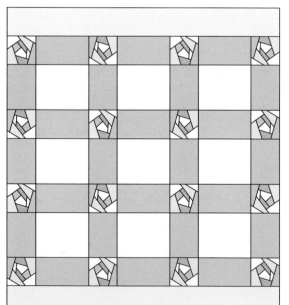

## Crazy Quilt Foundation Pattern

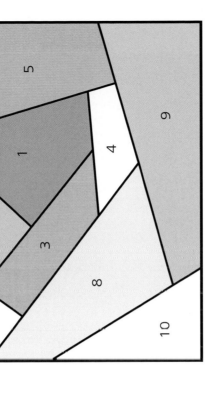

4. Sew a Crazy Quilt block to each end of horizontal blue floral strips; sew to top and bottom of quilt top. (**Diagram 5**)

5. Refer to Finishing, pages 138 to 142, to complete your quilt.

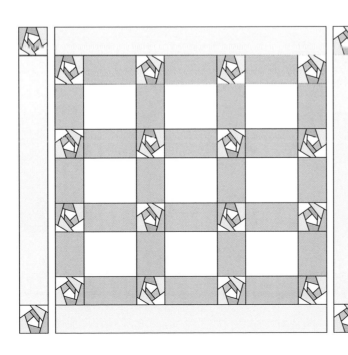

**Diagram 5**

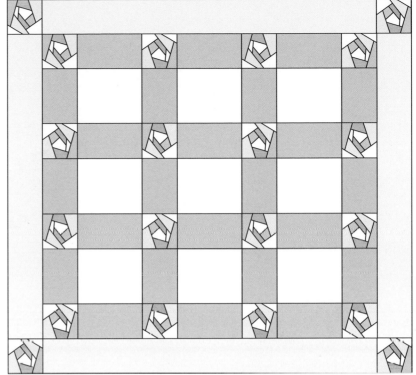

*Baby's Crazy Quilt Layout*

Time to Finish
16 hours

I wanted a quilt that was truly a little girl's quilt done in pinks with hearts and flowers, and this quilt is just that.

The method I used to make this quilt is a modern adaptation of the traditional postage stamp quilt where tiny patches of fabric—many the size of a postage stamp—were sewn together to create a picture. Some of those early quilts had thousands of little squares all painstakingly sewn by hand.

Today's quilter has the advantage of modern tools such as the rotary cutter and the sewing machine, but the crowning achievement has been the invention of fusible gridded interfacing. Now instead of sewing each seam individually, all of the squares of fabric are put into position as if you were working a jigsaw puzzle. Then the longer seams with many squares can be stitched. A few more seams, and the entire quilt is finished in a few hours rather than many, many days.

# Hearts and Flowers Postage Stamps

**APPROXIMATE SIZE**
43½" x 55½"

**TECHNIQUES**
Fusible Interfacing

**MATERIALS**
½ yard each of 4 different pink prints
1 yard white
1 yard pink print (border and binding)
3 yards backing
Batting
3 yards fusible interfacing grid (Pellon™® or June Tailor)

**CUTTING**
Quilt Center
311 squares, 2" x 2", white
514 squares, 2" x 2", pink prints (photographed quilt uses four different pink prints)

Finishing
5 strips, 3½"-wide strips, pink print (border)
4 squares, 3½" x 3½", white (cornerstones)
5 strips, 2½"-wide strips, pink print (binding)

# INSTRUCTIONS

## Quilt Center

1. For easier handling, cut fusible interfacing grid into two pieces—one that is 15 squares by 25 squares and one that is 18 squares by 25 squares. (**Diagram 1**)

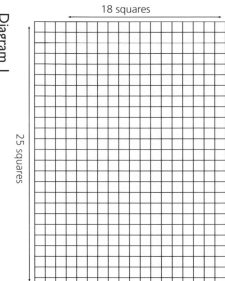

18 squares

25 squares

15 squares

25 squares

Diagram 1

2. Place first piece of interfacing bumpy (fusible) side up on a flat ironing surface. Referring to the Chart on page 125, position squares on interfacing with edges of squares butting up against each other. Fuse squares in place following manufacturer's instructions. (**Diagram 2**)

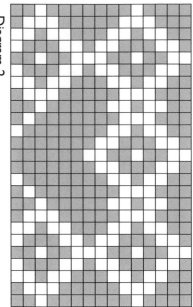

Diagram 2

3. Fold first vertical row of squares (on interfacing) right sides together with second row; sew along folded edge using a 1/4" seam allowance. (**Diagram 3**)

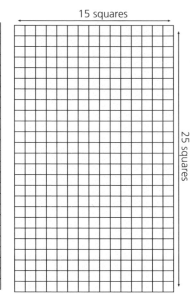

Diagram 3

4. Fold second vertical row right sides with third row; turn section so that interfacing is face up and sew along folded edge using a 1/4" seam allowance. (**Diagram 4**)

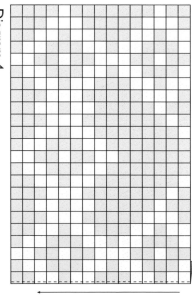

Diagram 4

5. Continue sewing in same manner until all vertical rows are sewn. (**Diagram 5**)

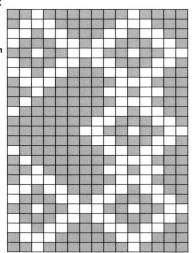

Diagram 5

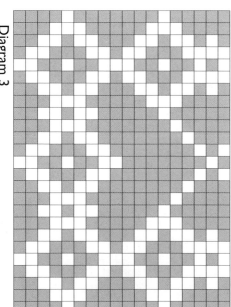

8. Referring to chart on page 125, repeat steps 2 to 6 with second piece of interfacing grid and remaining squares. (Diagram 8)

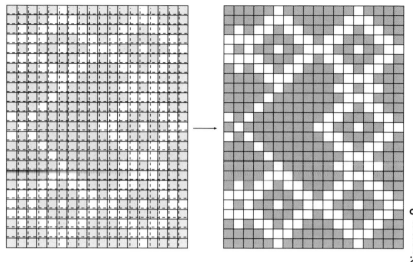

Diagram 8

6. Snip seams where horizontal rows meet and press seams for adjacent rows in opposite directions. (Diagram 6)

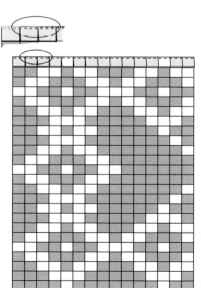

Diagram 6

7. Fold first horizontal row right sides together with second horizontal row. **Note:** *Be sure seams are going in opposite directions to reduce bulk.* Sew along fold using a ¹/₄" seam allowance. Repeat until all horizontal rows are sewn. (Diagram 7)

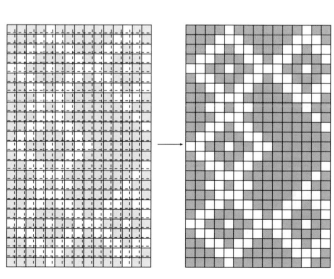

Diagram 7

## Finishing

1. Sew the two sections together. Press quilt top.

2. Measure quilt lengthwise and crosswise; cut two 3 1/2"-wide pink print strips to the lengthwise length and two 3 1/2"-wide pink print strips to the crosswise length. Sew lengthwise strips to sides of quilt. Sew 3 1/2" white squares to each end of crosswise strips. Sew to top and bottom of quilt. (**Diagram 9**)

3. Refer to Finishing, pages 138 to 142, to complete your quilt.

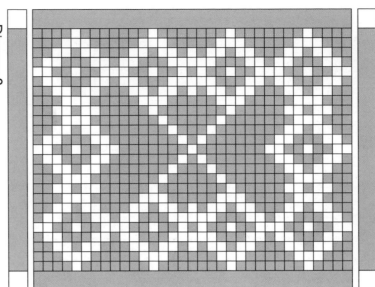

**Diagram 9**

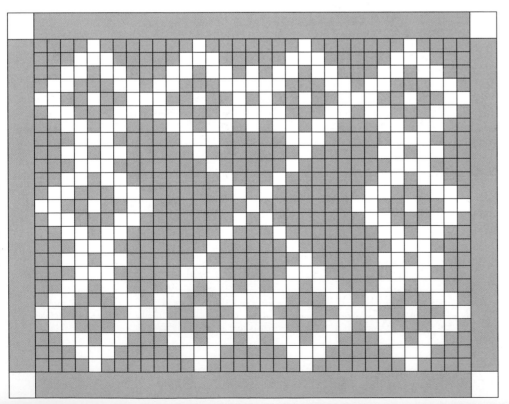

*Hearts and Flowers Postage Stamps Quilt Layout*

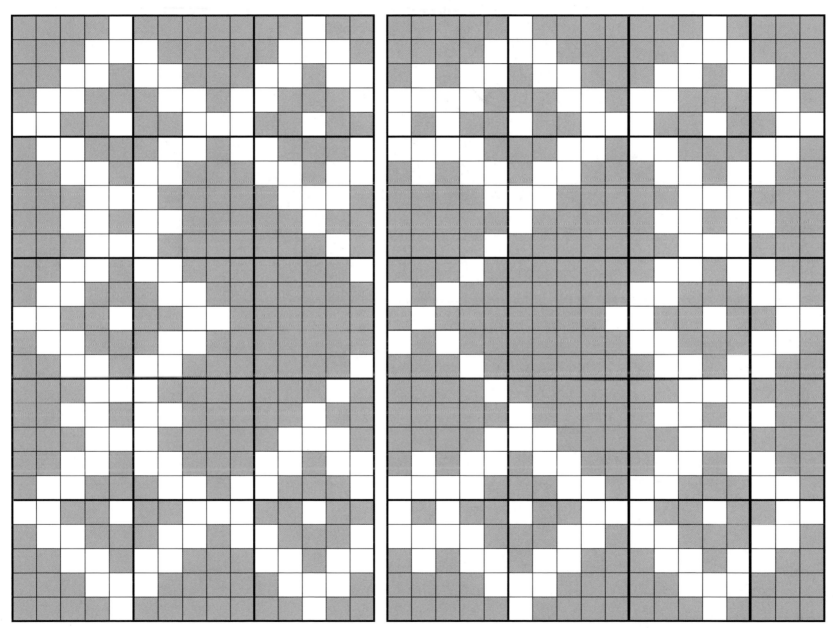

Chart for *Hearts and Flowers Postage Stamps*

Time to Finish
16 hours

# Sports Balls Postage Stamps

**APPROXIMATE SIZE**
43½" x 55½"

**TECHNIQUES**
Fusible Interfacing

**MATERIALS**
1⅛ yards medium blue
½ yard brown
¾ yard white
¼ yard red
¼ yard black
½ yard dark blue
1 yard red print (border, binding)
3 yards backing
Batting
3 yards fusible interfacing grid (Pellon™® or June Tailor)

**CUTTING**
**Quilt Center**

322 squares, 2" x 2", medium blue
104 squares, 2" x 2", brown
216 squares, 2" x 2", white
24 squares, 2" x 2", red
56 squares, 2" x 2", black
104 squares, 2" x 2", dark blue

**Finishing**

5 strips, 3½"-wide strips, red print (border)
5 strips, 2½"-wide strips, red print (binding)

---

*Since I made the Hearts and Flowers Postage Stamps quilt for a little girl, I felt I had to make a quilt for a little boy.*

*I decided to use the same modern adaptation of the traditional postage stamp quilt, using the fusible gridded interfacing as I did for the little girl's quilt.*

*In the traditional postage stamp quilt, thousands of tiny patches of fabric—many the size of a postage stamp—were sewn together to create a picture. Today's quilter has the advantage of being able to work with fusible gridded interfacing. Instead of sewing each piece individually, all of the squares are placed on the grid and sewn in long seams.*

*In this quilt, each sports ball is created with 2" x 2" pieces of fabric placed on the grid in much the same way as a jigsaw puzzle would be put together. Rather than a mere labor of love, this quilt is a "labor" of fun!*

*What little sports fan wouldn't be delighted to sleep under this quilt.*

# INSTRUCTIONS

## Quilt Center

1. For easier handling, cut fusible interfacing grid into two pieces, one that is 15 squares by 25 squares and one that is 18 squares by 25 squares. (**Diagram 1**)

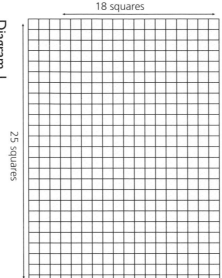

**Diagram 1**

18 squares

15 squares

25 squares

25 squares

**Diagram 2**

2. Place first piece of interfacing bumpy (fusible) side up on a flat ironing surface. Referring to chart on page 131, position squares on interfacing with edges of squares butting up against each other. Fuse squares in place following manufacturer's instructions. (**Diagram 2**)

3. Fold first vertical row of squares (on interfacing) right sides together with second row; sew along folded edge using a ¹/₄" seam allowance. (**Diagram 3**)

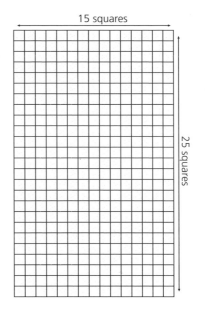

**Diagram 3**

4. Fold second vertical row right sides with third row; turn section so that interfacing is face up and sew along folded edge using a ¹/₄" seam allowance. (**Diagram 4**)

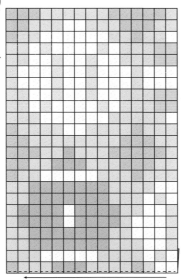

**Diagram 4**

5. Continue sewing in same manner until all vertical rows are sewn. (**Diagram 5**)

**Diagram 5**

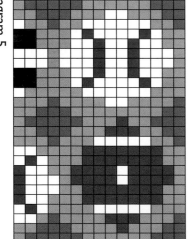

8. Referring to chart on page 131, repeat steps 2 to 6 with second piece of interfacing grid and remaining squares. (**Diagram 8**)

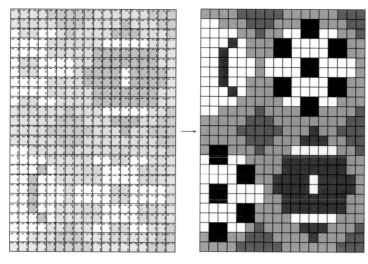

Diagram 8

6. Snip seams where horizontal rows meet and press seams for adjacent rows in opposite directions. (**Diagram 6**)

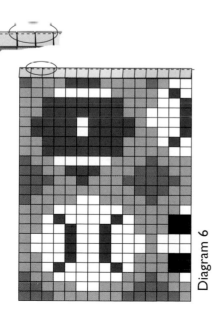

Diagram 6

7. Fold first horizontal row right sides together with second horizontal row. **Note:** *Be sure seams are going in opposite directions to reduce bulk.* Sew along fold using a 1/4" seam allowance. Repeat until all horizontal rows are sewn. (**Diagram 7**)

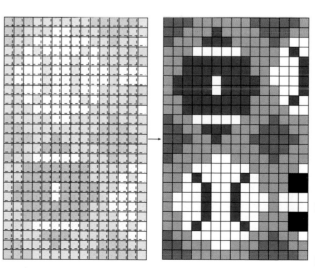

Diagram 7

*Finishing*

1. Sew sections together. Press quilt top.

2. Measure quilt lengthwise; cut two 3 1/2"-wide red print strips to that. Sew to sides of quilt. Measure quilt crosswise; cut two 3 1/2"-wide red print strips to that length. Sew to top and bottom of quilt.

3. Refer to Finishing, pages 138 to 142, to complete your quilt.

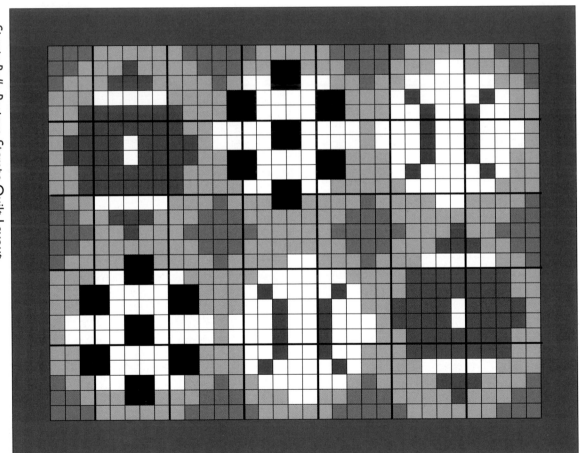

Sports Balls Postage Stamps Quilt Layout

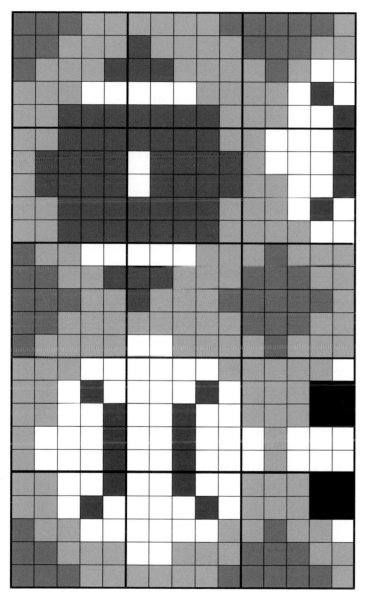
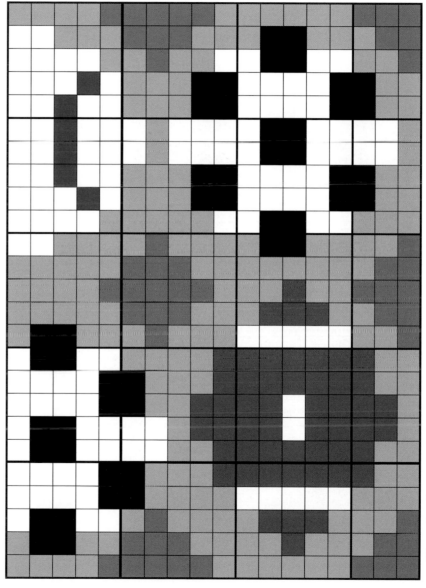

Chart for Sports Balls Postage Stamps Quilt

# General Directions

## BEFORE YOU BEGIN—A WORD ABOUT FABRIC

For over a hundred years, quilts have been made with 100% cotton fabric, and this remains today the fabric of choice for most quilters.

There are many properties in cotton that make it especially well suited to quiltmaking. There is less distortion in cotton fabric, thereby affording the quilter greater security in making certain that even the smallest bits of fabric will fit together. Because a quilt block made of cotton can be ironed flat with a steam iron, a puckered area, created by mistake, can be fixed. The sewing machine needle can move through cotton with a great deal of ease when compared to some synthetic fabrics. While you may find that quilt artists today often use other kinds of fabric to create the quilts quickly and accurately, 100% cotton is strongly recommended.

Cotton fabric today is produced in so many wonderful and exciting combinations of prints and solids that it is often difficult to pick colors for your quilt. We've chosen our favorite colors for these quilts, but don't be afraid to make your own choices

For years, quilters were advised to prewash all of their fabric to test for colorfastness and shrinkage. Now most quilters don't bother to prewash all of their fabric but they do pretest. Cut a strip about 2" wide from each piece of fabric that you will use in your quilt. Measure both the length and the width of the strip. Then immerse it in a bowl of very hot water, using a separate bowl for each piece of fabric. Be especially concerned about reds and dark blues because they have a tendency to bleed if the initial dyeing was not done properly. If it's one of your favorite fabrics that's bleeding, you might be able to salvage the fabric. Try washing the fabric in very hot water until you've washed out all of the excess dye. Unfortunately, fabrics that continue to bleed after they have been washed repeatedly will bleed forever. So eliminate them right at the start.

Now, take each one of the strips and iron them dry with a hot iron. Be especially careful not to stretch the strip. When the strips are completely dry, measure and compare them to the size of your original strip. If all of your fabric is shrinking the same amount, you don't have to worry about uneven shrinkage in your quilt. When you wash the final

quilt, the puckering that will result may give you the look of an antique quilt. If you don't want this look, you are going to have to wash and dry all of your fabric before you start cutting. Iron the fabric using some spray starch or sizing to give the fabric a crisp finish.

If you are never planning to wash your quilt, i.e. your quilt is intended to be a wall hanging, you could eliminate the pre-testing process. You may run the risk, however, of some future relative to whom you have willed your quilts deciding that the wall hanging needs freshening by washing.

Before beginning to work, make sure that your fabric is absolutely square. If it is not, you will have difficulty cutting square pieces. Fabric is woven with crosswise and lengthwise threads. Lengthwise threads should be parallel to the selvage (that's the finished edge along the sides; sometimes the fabric company prints its name along the selvage), and crosswise threads should be perpendicular to the selvage. If fabric is off grain, you can usually straighten it by pulling gently on the true bias in the opposite direction to the off-grain edge. Continue doing this until the crosswise threads are at a right angle to the lengthwise threads.

## EASY APPLIQUÉ

Easy Appliqué is done using paper-backed fusible web rather than freezer paper or templates. There are many different paper-backed fusible products on the market today. Each has its own unique characteristics that will help you decide which to use when making a quilt. Always be sure to follow the manufacturer's directions as each product differs greatly.

For Easy Appliqué, it is best to use a lightweight fusible web such as HeatnBond Lite or Steam-a-Seam 2 Lite®. This will enable you to use a machine zigzag to appliqué the edges. Using a heavyweight brand will cause your needle to gum up and possibly break.

Trace the patterns onto the paper side of the fusible web following the manufacturer's directions. Be especially careful because pattern pieces that are not symmetrical will end up as mirror images of the finished project.

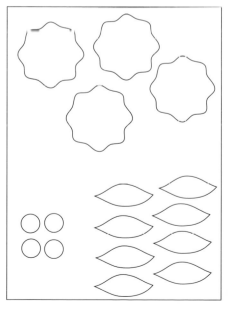

**Hint:** *Trace patterns that will be cut from the same fabric together, then rough-cut the whole group of patterns for one color from the fusible web.* (**Diagram 1**)

**Diagram 1**

Now position fusible web pattern or group of patterns with paper side up onto wrong side of fabric; fuse in place with hot iron. **Note:** *Refer to manufacturer's directions for heat setting and pressing time for the product you are using.*

Cut out the pattern pieces from the fusible web along the drawn lines. Keep paper on fabric until ready to use.

Remove paper and position the fabric appliqué pieces onto the block referring to the individual project instructions. Fuse in place.

Using a machine zigzag or blanket stitch and matching or invisible thread, stitch along all raw edges of appliqué. You may want to practice or another piece of fabric to see which zigzag width and length works best for you.

# FOUNDATION PIECING

## Materials

Before you begin, decide the kind of foundation on which you are planning to piece the blocks.

### Paper

The most popular choice is paper. It's readily available and fairly inexpensive. You can use copy paper, newsprint, tracing paper—even computer paper. The paper does not remain a permanent part of your quilt as it is removed once the blocks are completely sewn.

## Other Materials

Another option for foundation materials is Tear Away™ or Fun-dation™, translucent non-woven materials combining both the advantages of both paper and fabric. They are easy to see through, but like paper they can be removed with ease.

Currently a new kind of foundation material has appeared in the market place: a foundation paper that dissolves in water after use. Two companies, W.H. Collins and EZ Quilting by Wrights are producing this product.

## Preparing the Foundation

Place your foundation material over your chosen block and trace the block pattern. Use a ruler and a fine-line pencil or permanent marker, and make sure that all lines are straight. Sometimes short dashed lines or even dotted lines are easier to make. Be sure to copy all numbers. You will need to make a foundation for each block you are planning to use.

If you have a home copier, you can copy your tracing on the copy machine. Since the copy machine might slightly alter the measurements of the block, make certain that you copy each block from the original pattern.

You can also scan the block and then print out the required number of blocks.

## Cutting the Fabric

In foundation piecing, you do not have to cut perfect shapes! You can, therefore, use odd pieces of fabric: squares, strips, and rectangles. The one thing you must remember, however, is that every piece must be at least 1/4" larger on all sides than the space it is going to cover. Strips and squares are easy: just measure the length and width of the needed space and add 1/2" all around. Cut your strip to that measurement. Triangles, however, can be a bit tricky. In that case, measure the widest point of the triangle and cut your fabric about 1/2" to 1" wider.

## Other Supplies for Foundation Piecing

You will need a cleaned and oiled sewing machine, glue stick, pins, paper scissors, fabric scissors, and foundation material.

Before beginning to sew your actual block by machine, determine the proper stitch length. Use a

133

piece of the paper you are planning to use for the foundation and draw a straight line on it. Set your machine so that it sews with a fairly short stitch (about 20 stitches per inch). Sew along the line. If you can tear the paper apart with ease, you are sewing with the right length. You don't want to sew with such a short stitch that the paper falls apart by itself.

## Making the Foundation-Pieced Block

The important thing to remember about making a foundation block is that the fabric goes on the un-marked side of the foundation while you sew on the printed side. The finished block is a mirror image of the original pattern.

**Step 1:** Hold the foundation up to a light source—even a window pane—with the unmarked side facing. Find the space marked 1 on the un-marked side and put a dab of glue there. Place the fabric right side up on the unmarked side on Space 1, making certain that the fabric overlaps at least ¹/₄" on all sides of Space 1. (**Diagram 2**)

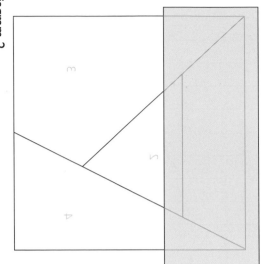

Diagram 2

**Step 2:** Fold the foundation along the line be-tween Space 1 and Space 2. Cut the fabric so that it is ¹/₄" from the fold. (**Diagram 3**)

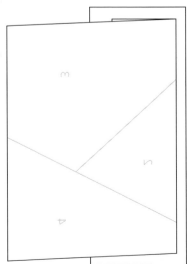

Diagram 3

**Step 3:** With right sides together, place Fabric Piece 2 on Fabric Piece 1, making sure that the edge of Piece 2 is even with the just-trimmed edge of Piece 1. (**Diagram 4**)

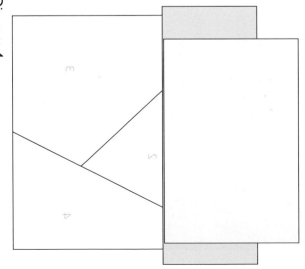

Diagram 4

**Hint:** *If you use a small stitch, it will be easier to remove the paper later. Start stitching about two or three stitches before the beginning of the line and end your sewing two or three stitches beyond the line, allowing the stitches to be held in place by the next round of stitching rather than by backstitching.*

**Step 6:** Turn the work over and open Piece 2. Finger press the seam open. (**Diagram 7**)

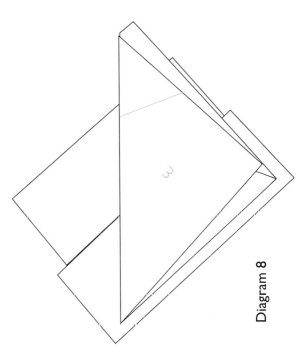

Diagram 7

**Step 7:** Turning the work so that the marked side is on top, fold the foundation forward along the line between Space 1+2 and Space 3. Trim about 1/8" to 1/4" from the fold. It is easier to trim the paper if you pull the paper away from the stitching. If you use fabric as your foundation, fold the fabric forward as far as it will go and then start to trim. (**Diagram 8**)

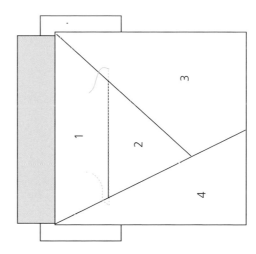

Diagram 8

**Step 4:** To make certain that Piece 2 will cover Space 2, fold the fabric piece back along the line between Space 1 and Space 2. (**Diagram 5**)

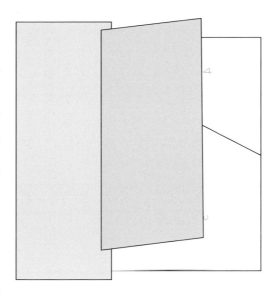

Diagram 5

**Step 5:** With the marked side of the foundation facing up, place the piece on the sewing machine (or sew by hand), holding both Piece 1 and Piece 2 in place. Sew along the line between Space 1 and Space 2. (**Diagram 6**)

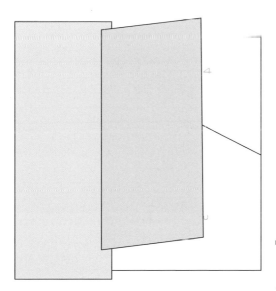

Diagram 6

**Step 8**: Place Fabric #3 right side down even with the just-trimmed edge. (**Diagram 9**)

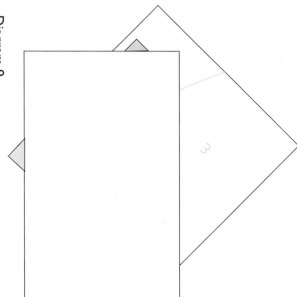

Diagram 9

**Step 10**: Turn the work over, open Piece 3 and finger press the seam. (**Diagram 11**)

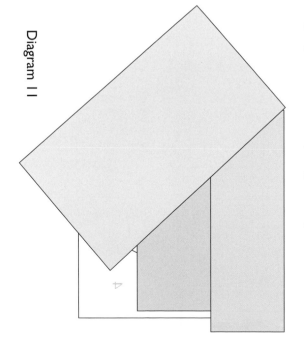

Diagram 11

Diagram 9

**Step 9**: Turn the block over to the marked side and sew along the line between Space 1+2 and Space 3. (**Diagram 10**)

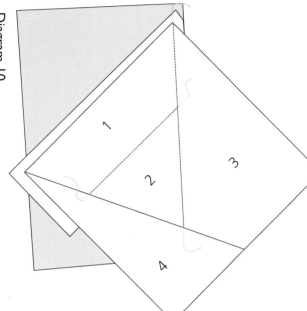

Diagram 10

**Step 11**: In the same way you have added the other pieces, add Piece #4 to complete this block. Trim the fabric ¼" from the edge of the foundation. (**Diagram 12**)

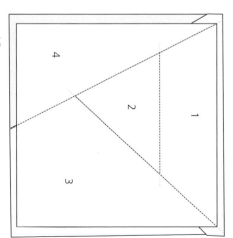

Diagram 12

The foundation-pieced block is completed.
(Diagram 13)

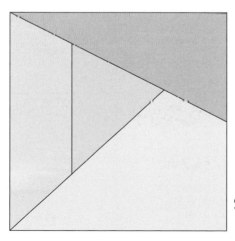

**Diagram 13**

of the top section to the corners of the bottom section. (Diagram 14)

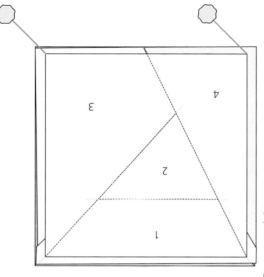

**Diagram 14**

After you have finished sewing a block, don't immediately remove the paper. Since you are often piecing with tiny bits of fabric, grainline is not a factor. Therefore, some of the pieces may have been cut on the bias and may have a tendency to stretch. You can eliminate any problem with distortion by keeping the paper in place until all of the blocks have been sewn together. If, however, you want to remove the paper, stay stitch along the outer edge of the block to help keep the block in shape.

*Sewing Multiple Sections*

Many of the blocks in foundation piecing are created with two or more sections. These sections, which are indicated by letters, are individually pieced and then sewn together. The cutting line for these sections is indicated by a bold line. Before you start to make any of these multi-section blocks, begin by cutting the foundation piece apart so that each section is worked independently. Leave a ¼" seam allowance around each section.

**Step 1:** Following the instructions above for Making the Block, complete each section. Then place the sections right side together. Pin the corners

**Step 2:** If you are certain that the pieces are aligned correctly, sew the two sections together using the regular stitch length on the sewing machine.

**Step 3:** Press the sections open and continue sewing the sections in pairs. **(Diagram 15)**

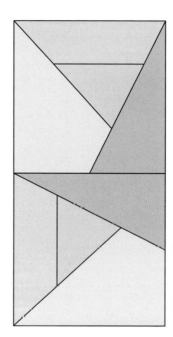

**Diagram 15**

**Step 4:** Sew necessary pairs of sections together to complete the block. (**Diagram 16**) The blocks are now ready to sew into your quilt.

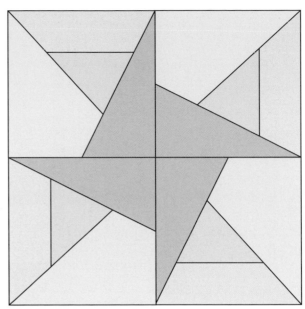

Diagram 16

*What You Don't Want to Forget*

1. If you plan to sew by hand, begin by taking some backstitches that will anchor the thread at the beginning of the line. Then use a backstitch every four of five stitches. End the stitching with a few backstitches.

2. If you plan to sew by machine, start stitching two or three stitches before the start of the stitching line and finish your stitching two or three stitches beyond the end.

3. Use a short stitch (about 20 stitches per inch) for paper foundations to make it easier to remove the paper. If the paper falls apart as you sew, your stitches are too short.

4. Finger press (or use an iron) each seam as you finish it.

5. Stitching which goes from a space into another space will not interfere with adding additional fabric pieces.

6. Remember to trim all seam allowances about 1/4".

Diagram 17

7. When sewing points, start from the wide end and sew towards the point.

8. Unless you plan to use it only once in the block, it is a good idea to stay away from directional prints in foundation piecing.

9. When cutting pieces for foundation piecing, never worry about the grainline.

10. Always remember to sew on the marked side, placing the fabric on the unmarked side.

11. Follow the numerical order, or it won't work.

12. Once you have finished making a block do not remove the paper until the entire quilt has been finished unless you stay stitch around the outside of the block.

13. Be sure that the ink you use to make your foundation is permanent and will not wash out into your fabric.

# FINISHING YOUR QUILT

*Simple Borders*

To add your borders, measure the quilt top lengthwise and cut two border strips to that length by the width measurement given in the instructions. Strips may have to be pieced to achieve the correct length.

To make the joining seam less noticeable, sew the strips together diagonally. Place two strips right sides together at right angles. Sew a diagonal seam. (**Diagram 17**)

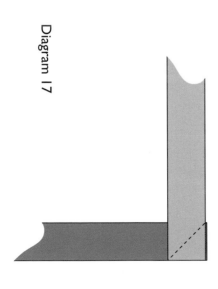

Trim excess fabric ¼" from stitching. (Diagram 18)

**Diagram 18**

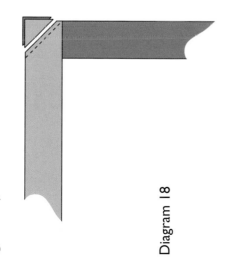

Press seam open. (Diagram 19)

**Diagram 19**

Sew strips to the sides of the quilt. Press toward border. Now measure the quilt top crosswise, being sure to include the borders you have just added. Cut two border strips to that length, following the width measurement given in the instructions.

Add these borders to the top and bottom of the quilt.

Repeat this process for any additional borders. Use the ¼" seam allowance at all times and press all of the seams toward the border just added. Press the quilt top carefully.

*Attaching the Batting and Backing*

There are a number of different types of batting on the market today including the new fusible battings that eliminate the need for basting. Your choice of batting will depend upon how you are planning to use your quilt. If the quilt is to serve as a wall hanging, you will probably want to use a thin cotton batting. A quilt made with a thin cotton or cotton/polyester blend works best for machine quilting. Very thick polyester batting should be used only for tied quilts.

The best fabric for quilt backing is 100% cotton fabric. If your quilt is larger than the available fabric, you will have to piece your backing fabric. When joining the fabric, try not to have a seam going down the center. Instead cut off the selvages and make a center strip that is about 36" wide and have narrower strips at the sides. Seam the pieces together and carefully iron the seams open. (This is one of the few times in making a quilt that a seam should be pressed open.) Several fabric manufacturers are now selling fabric in 90" or 108"-widths for use as backing fabric.

It is a good idea to remove the batting from its wrapping 24 hours before you plan to use it and open it out to full size. You will find that the batting will now lie flat when you are ready to use it.

The batting and the backing should be cut about one to two inches larger on all sides than the quilt top. Place the backing wrong side up on a flat surface. Smooth out the batting on top of this, matching the outer edges. Center the quilt top, right side up, on top of the batting.

Now the quilt layers must be held together before quilting, and there are several methods for doing this:

**Safety-pin Basting:** Starting from the center and working toward the edges, pin through all layers at one time with large safety pins. The pins should be placed no more than 4" apart. As you work, think of your quilting plan to make sure that the pins will avoid prospective quilting lines.

**Thread Basting:** Baste the three layers together with long stitches. Start in the center and sew toward the edges in a number of diagonal lines.

**Quilt-gun Basting:** This handy trigger tool pushes nylon tags through all layers of the quilt. Start in the center and work toward the outside edges. The tags should be placed about 4" apart. You can sew right over the tags, which can then be easily removed by cutting them off with scissors.

**Spray or Heat-set Basting:** Several manufacturers have spray adhesives available especially for quilters. Apply these products by following the manufacturers' directions. You might want to test these products before you use them to make sure that they meet your requirements.

**Fusible Iron-on Batting:** These battings are a wonderful new way to hold quilt layers together without using any of the other time-consuming methods of basting. Again, you will want to test these battings to be certain that you are happy with the results. Follow the manufacturers' directions.

## Quilting

If you like the process of hand quilting, you can—of course—finish these projects by hand quilting. However, if you want to finish these quilts quickly, you might want to use a sewing machine for quilting.

If you have never used a sewing machine for quilting, you may want to find a book and read about the technique. You do not need a special machine for quilting. Just make sure that your machine has been oiled and is in good working condition.

If you are going to do machine quilting, you should invest in an even-feed foot. This foot is designed to feed the top and bottom layers of a quilt evenly through the machine. The foot prevents puckers from forming as you machine quilt. Use a fine transparent nylon thread or thread that matches the background in the top and regular sewing thread in the bobbin.

**Quilting in the ditch** is one of the easiest ways to machine quilt. This is a term used to describe stitching along the seam line between two pieces of fabric. Using your fingers, pull the blocks or pieces apart slightly and machine stitch right between the two pieces. The stitching will look better if you keep the stitching to the side of the seam that does not have the extra bulk of the seam under it. The quilting will be hidden in the seam.

**Free-form machine quilting** can be used to quilt around a design or to quilt a motif. The quilting is done with a darning foot and the feed dogs down on the sewing machine. It takes practice to master free-form quilting because you are controlling the movement of the quilt under the needle rather than the sewing machine moving the quilt. You can quilt in any direction – up and down, side-to-side, and even

in circles – without pivoting the quilt around the needle. Practice this quilting method before trying it on your quilt.

## Attaching the Continuous Machine Binding

Once the quilt has been quilted, it must be bound to cover the raw edges.

**Step 1:** Start by trimming the backing and batting even with the quilt top. Measure the quilt top and cut enough 2½"-wide strips to go around all four sides of the quilt plus 12". Join the strips end to end with diagonal seams and trim the corners. Press the seams open. (**Diagram 20**)

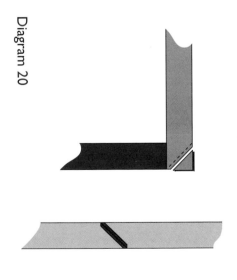

Diagram 20

**Step 2:** Cut one end of the strip at a 45-degree angle and press under ¼". (**Diagram 21**)

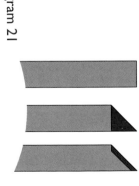

Diagram 21

**Step 3:** Press entire strip in half lengthwise, wrong sides together. **(Diagram 22)**

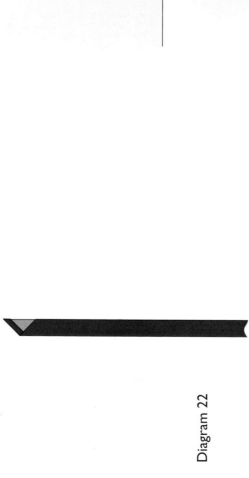

Diagram 22

**Step 4:** On the back of the quilt, position the binding in the middle of one side, keeping the raw edges together. Sew the binding to the quilt with the ¼" seam allowance, beginning about three inches below the folded end of the binding. At the corner, stop ¼" from the edge of the quilt and backstitch. **(Diagram 23)**

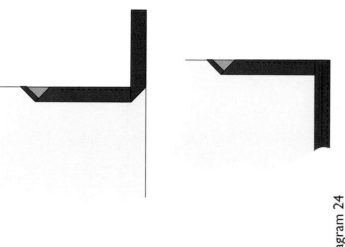

Diagram 23

**Step 5:** Fold binding away from quilt so it is at a right angle to edge just sewn. Then, fold the binding back on itself so the fold is on the quilt edge and the raw edges are aligned with the adjacent side

of the quilt. Begin sewing at the quilt edge. **(Diagram 24)**

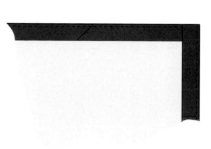

Diagram 24

**Step 6:** Continue in the same way around the remaining sides of the quilt. Stop about 2" away from the starting point. Trim any excess binding and tuck it inside the folded end. Finish the stitching. **(Diagram 25)**

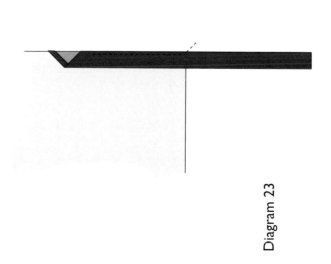

Diagram 25

**Step 7:** Fold the binding to the front of the quilt so the seam line is covered; machine-stitch the binding in place on the front of the quilt. Use a straight stitch or tiny zigzag with invisible or matching thread. If you have a sewing machine that does embroidery stitches, you may want to use your favorite stitch.

*Adding a Rod Pocket*

In order to hang your quilt for family and friends to enjoy, you will need to attach a rod pocket to the back.

**Step 1:** Cut a strip of fabric, 6" wide by the width of the quilt.

**Step 2:** Fold short ends of strip under ¹/₄", then fold another ¹/₄". Sew along first fold. (**Diagram 26**)

Diagram 26

**Step 3:** Fold strip lengthwise with wrong sides together. Sew along raw edges with a ¹/₄" seam allowance to form a long tube. (**Diagram 27**)

Diagram 27

**Step 4:** Place tube on ironing surface with seam up and centered; press seam open and folds flat. (Diagram 28)

Diagram 28

142

**Step 5:** Place tube on back of quilt, seam side against quilt, about 1" from top edge and equal distant from side edges. (**Diagram 29**) Pin in place so tube is straight across quilt.

Diagram 29

**Step 6:** Hand stitch top and bottom edges of tube to back of quilt being careful not to let stitches show on front of quilt.

*Labeling Your Quilt*

Always sign and date your quilt when finished. You can make a label by cross-stitching or embroidering or even writing on a label with a permanent marking pen on the back of your quilt. If you are friends with your computer, you can even create an attractive label on the computer.

# Index

## METRIC EQUIVALENTS

| inches | cm | inches | cm | inches | cm |
|---|---|---|---|---|---|
| 1 | 2.54 | 11 | 27.94 | 21 | 53.34 |
| 2 | 5.08 | 12 | 30.48 | 22 | 55.88 |
| 3 | 7.62 | 13 | 33.02 | 23 | 58.42 |
| 4 | 10.16 | 14 | 35.56 | 24 | 60.96 |
| 5 | 12.70 | 15 | 38.10 | 30 | 76.20 |
| 6 | 15.24 | 16 | 40.64 | 36 | 91.44 |
| 7 | 17.78 | 17 | 43.18 | 42 | 106.68 |
| 8 | 20.32 | 18 | 45.72 | 48 | 121.92 |
| 9 | 22.86 | 19 | 48.26 | 54 | 137.16 |
| 10 | 25.40 | 20 | 50.8 | 60 | 152.40 |